PRAISE FOR

Master the Media

"Media literacy is an essential subject for life in the twenty-first century, and Julie Smith has written an essential guide."

—JACK LULE, Professor and Chair of Journalism and Communication, Lehigh University

"As our experience of media evolves from mere reception to active participation, learning to think critically about content is not enough. We must learn to act purposefully with these new tools lest they, and the people behind them, act purposefully on us, instead. In an era when nothing short of true mastery will do, Julie Smith gives parents and educators clear and simple steps for how to become media literate in the twenty-first century."

—DOUGLAS RUSHKOFF, Author, *Present Shock: When Everything Happens Now*

"We must become more media-aware in our daily lives! Julie Smith's all-inclusive guide to exploring media literacy should be required reading for every parent and educator in this digital age."

—JERRY BLUMENGARTEN, @cybraryman1, Connected Educator, Speaker, Writer

"*Master the Media* is a powerful resource that all educators and parents should read to make us better aware of media's 24/7 impact on us as consumers. Julie Smith's insight into the world of media literacy had me thinking, from the very first chapter, of our responsibility, as parents and as educators, to help our children evaluate all forms of media for truth and authenticity. This book will make you reflect on how our world continues to evolve because of technology and how it influences our lives on a daily basis."

—JIMMY CASAS, Award-winning Principal, Speaker and Co-author, *What Connected Educators Do Differently*

"This book is for everyone who recognizes the power of the media, and wants to know how that power is used and what we need to do to master media literacy skills. Julie Smith explains why those of us who promote media literacy education really are in it to save the world."

—ERIN MCNEILL, Founder and President, Media Literacy Now

"As a parent, an educator, and as an informed citizen, I found *Master the Media* to be a fascinating and eye-opening read on the importance of media literacy. Julie Smith expertly unfolds the history of the media around us, while providing tools to help us become leaders of media literacy. A must read for every household!"

—BETH HOUF, Middle School Principal

"Education of media should not be an elective within our learning environments; education of media should be a pre-requisite within primary education and a measured goal of literacy as a student progresses through secondary education. Considering how much influence media has on children and their cultural experiences, laying a foundation of critical judgment of media for children should become an objective for every educator in the world. This book can help that process within our communities."

—JESSE MILLER, New Media and Social Media Educator, MediatedReality.com

"Julie Smith manages to make the important—but all too often, frighteningly dull—topic of media literacy interesting. Her book is full of good examples and smart, engaging exercises designed to make all of us critical, informed viewers of modern media culture."

—JUDD SLIVKA, Assistant Professor of Convergence Journalism, University of Missouri School of Journalism

"*Master the Media* is an important book, directed at parents and others who are in positions to influence the media habits of young people. The book takes a very personal approach to the constructive use of the media, offering support and direction, so that individuals can develop a healthy independence from the messages they receive through the media."

—ART SILVERBLATT, Author,
Media Literacy: Keys to Interpreting Media Messages

MASTER THE MEDIA:

How Teaching Media Literacy Can Save Our Plugged-In World

by Julie Smith

Master the Media

© 2015 by Julie Smith

This book is available at special discounts when purchased in quantity for use as premiums, promotions, fundraising, and educational use. For inquiries and details, contact us: shelley@daveburgessconsulting.com.

Published by Dave Burgess Consulting, Inc.
San Diego, CA
http://daveburgessconsulting.com

Cover Design by Genesis Kohler
Editing and Interior Design by My Writers' Connection

Library of Congress Control Number: 2015944519
Paperback ISBN: 978-0-9861554-4-4
Ebook ISBN: 978-0-9861554-5-1

First Printing: July 2015

Dedication

For all my Smiths
and all my Julies

Thank you...

Dave Burgess, for leaning across a table one night and saying, "You've got a book in you." And to his better half, Shelley, who held my hand professionally, personally, and sisterly throughout the entire process.

Erin Casey, for making me sound more interesting than I really am.

Jack Lule, Patrick Murphy, and Cynthia Cooper, for being my first and favorite media professors.

Art Silverblatt, for inspiring and influencing my career like no one else. He is my Fairy Godprofessor, and I adore him.

Mary Kienstra, Heidi Jones, Jim Werner, and Doug Robertson, for assisting in various stages of this project.

Carla Nieman, for planting a seed a few years ago.

Ellen Stimson, for sharing her secrets.

Mark Stevison, for saving a hard drive and my spirit one Monday afternoon.

Julie Korenak, Julie Hoevelmann, Julie Dibble, Julie Knost, Julie Heuer, and Julie Griffey, for being my Julies.

Norm Nilsson, for providing unwavering optimism and constant cheerleading.

I love that Don Goble, Heather Melton, Tim Kohler, Tyann Cherry, Candice Fee, Ashley Cramer, Krystal Wilson, and Blake Nichols were so willing to share their passion for media literacy in this book.

Ian, Jack, and Sean, please make sure you marry someone who will still let you hang out with us occasionally.

And Tom Nilsson? Don't worry. I will always remember that you did this first.

Contents

Why I Wrote this Book

Certain moments of life get indelibly carved into our memories. One of those moments in my life happened when I discovered the career I really wanted. Twenty years ago, while talking on the phone with a former professor and trying to figure out what to do with my life, I said, "I want to teach people how to watch TV."

His reply was short: "You're talking about media literacy."

I had never heard the term before. But since that moment, media literacy has been the focus of my professional life.

When I tell people what I teach, I usually have to offer a follow-up explanation. The term is unfamiliar to people, but when I describe my work, I am greeted with nods of agreement. So, when someone asks what I do, my response sounds something like this:

"I teach people to critically view all the media they consume. How to evaluate it, critique it, and analyze it, so they're not sheep, but think for themselves, instead. So they make smart decisions about purchasing and voting, and so they don't believe the stereotypes presented to them."

Yes, it would be much easier to say, "I teach geometry." People understand that. They value it. They know where it fits into a school landscape. Media literacy is a different animal. It truly is cross-curricular and important for every age and every subject. It's not a topic; it's a skill.

Why should we study the media? They're pervasive and persuasive. They affect us emotionally. We vote, buy, and live by their suggestions. They take up our time. They present the world to us. But how often do we stand back and ask what it all *means*?

Last year, I did a presentation called "Media Literacy to Save the World." My father was skeptical and questioned the title's claim. But if we were savvy media consumers, the world would be a different place. We *can* change the world through media literacy, and we need to start with the young people in our lives.

If you're a teacher, you will find media literacy woven into several of the Common Core College and Career Readiness Anchor Standards. These standards may not use the phrase "media literacy," but take a look:

- Integrate and evaluate content presented in diverse media and formats (Reading Standard 7).[1]
- Evaluate information presented in diverse media (Speaking and Listening 2).[2]
- Assess the credibility and accuracy of sources (Writing 8).[3]

If you're a parent, teaching your children media literacy will help them learn to think for themselves and be aware of the media around them. They will become discerning media consumers—liking what deserves to be liked and ignoring what deserves to be ignored.

Think of it this way: media literacy is critical thinking, and critical thinking is good for us. However, the sheer volume of media messages will most likely only *increase*. No one would disagree that analyzing the constant flow of media messages is a bad idea. But *when* and *how* to add media literacy to an already busy schedule can seem daunting. My goal for this book is to help you with the *when*, the *how*, and especially the *why*—so you can start *now*.

QR CODES

**Common Core
Anchor Standards**

**Media Use Statistics
–Compiled by Frank Baker**

**Media References in
Common Core Standards
–From Frank Baker**

FOOTNOTES

[1] "English Language Arts Standards » Anchor Standards » College and Career Readiness Anchor Standards for Reading," *Common Core State Standards Initiative*, accessed June 13, 2015, http://www.corestandards.org/ELA-Literacy/CCRA/R/#CCSS. ELA-Literacy.CCRA.R.7.

[2] "English Language Arts Standards » Anchor Standards » College and Career Readiness Anchor Standards for Speaking and Listening," *Common Core State Standards Initiative*, accessed June 13, 2015, http://www.corestandards.org/ELA-Literacy/CCRA/SL/#CCSS.ELA-Literacy.CCRA.SL.2.

[3] "English Language Arts Standards » Anchor Standards » College and Career Readiness Anchor Standards for Writing," *Common Core State Standards Initiative*, accessed June 13, 2015, http://www.corestandards.org/ELA-Literacy/CCRA/W/#CCSS. ELA-Literacy.CCRA.W.8.

1

LET'S DO THIS

FACTS TO REMEMBER:

- ☛ Media outlets are owned by profit-seeking corporations.
- ☛ They create and perpetuate our culture.
- ☛ The time we spend with media keeps increasing.
- ☛ Media literacy is NOT media bashing.

Studies predict that, by 2015, the average American will consume more than fifteen hours of media each day, *in addition to* the media they view at work time.[1] If you're thinking the math doesn't add up, you're right. Fifteen hours sounds impossible. But media researchers are savvy to the fact that we often use more than one medium at a time. For example, you might be reading this book in front of the television or while listening to music. That would count as double media usage. If only our sleep could be as productive!

Media themselves are neither good nor bad; they're simply tools that deliver content. But because we spend so much time with media, they deserve to be studied, analyzed, and scrutinized. It's important to understand how the content and the rate at which we consume it impact our lives. How does media usage affect us? How is it affecting students?

Researchers insist that too much media consumption can lead to obesity, lower school achievement, aggression, and even rudeness. Fifteen hours of daily consumption most surely makes an impact. Scholars in Canada began studying the effect of media consumption forty years ago. Their interest in the effects of media had a nationalism angle. The study determined that, because so many Canadians receive American media and pop culture, it is important for them to consume media critically to maintain their unique national identity.[2,3]

The term "media literacy" has been around for years, with various definitions. Most of the definitions include the words *analyze, critique,* and *evaluate.* And with schools emphasizing critical thinking, who could argue with those verbs?

Sometimes media literacy is described as "trying to teach the fish that water exists." How do you make kids aware of the role the media play in their lives? They constantly swim in this water of media messages where they are learning about relationships, marriage, love, sex, divorce, friendship, health, identity, and consumerism. They are learning what it means to be handsome, beautiful, and successful, and they are learning about products that will fix their implied inadequacies.

By engaging in this online world, they learn about education, politics, wars, riots, protests, and debates. And they see victories, celebrations, sportsmanship, talent, and citizenship. They see inspiring heroes, athletes, and characters. Media expose them to people, countries, and situations that they might never experience in person. So to claim that the media are harmful is a gross overgeneralization. Yet, to claim media should not be analyzed is a naïve mistake.

Even though many media productions are created specifically to entertain, they educate as well—but not always accurately. Thousands of studies have reviewed the relationship between media consumption and our perceptions of "reality." You've likely witnessed this break with reality firsthand: the student who thinks everyone in Africa lives in a hut or the friend who shares an obviously doctored photo on social media. We are reared and educated in a mediated world.

A wide range of issues pervades our mass media. But we cannot change the messages of the media because their creators enjoy First Amendment protection. Therefore, the obvious way to avoid any potentially negative consequences of the "big bad media" is to become media literate. And as teachers, we must educate the *receivers* of the messages.

When I tell people I teach media literacy, many assume I am anti-media. That couldn't be further from the truth! A food critic doesn't hate food. In fact, a food critic has a great love for and fascination with food. He examines how it is produced and presented. He evaluates the taste, color, smell, and texture of the food. A food critic appreciates a wonderful meal for all of those reasons. But he also notices deficiencies in the dish that others might miss. Similarly, my teaching media literacy doesn't mean I hate the media. It means I analyze their production, presentation, effect, and yes—their "taste."

The purpose of media literacy education is to help individuals of all ages develop the necessary habits of inquiry and skills of expression to be critical thinkers, effective communicators, and active citizens in today's world. The National Association for Media Literacy Education (NAMLE) lists the following core principles that should be familiar to anyone instructing others in media literacy:

- Media Literacy Education requires active inquiry and critical thinking about the messages we receive and create.

- It expands the concept of literacy to include all forms of media (i.e., reading and writing).

- Media Literacy Education builds and reinforces skills for learners of all ages. Like print literacy, those skills necessitate integrated, interactive, and repeated practice.

- It develops informed, reflective, and engaged participants essential for a democratic society.

- Media Literacy Education recognizes that media are a part of culture and function as agents of socialization.

- It affirms that people use their individual skills, beliefs, and experiences to construct their own meanings from media messages.[4]

The importance of being media literate is hard to debate. In fact, media literacy courses are required in countries such as Great Britain, Canada, Australia, and Spain. However, media literacy has had a tough road in the United States. Although many agree on its importance, there is no consensus on where or when it should be taught. School schedules are already full; can we really ask teachers to do *one more thing*?

Using media literacy in the classroom goes beyond a teacher showing a YouTube clip or using iPads. The next generation needs to have some context for the media they consume. As educators and parents, we can impress upon them the value of asking:

- What's the history?
- Who's creating these messages?
- Who makes money from these messages?
- How are they involved in the process?
- What is the point of viewing the message?

The road to media literacy can begin anywhere—not just in the library. Simple questions can help children not only become aware of the media's presence but its influence as well.

I hope this book will make it easier for you to help the children in your life become critical consumers of the media. Being media literate is a twenty-first-century survival skill. Our children need it not only to navigate the world in which they currently live but also the mediated world of the future.

While *Master the Media* isn't comprehensive, it provides a good starting point for anyone interested in helping others become critical consumers in today's always-on culture. I've segmented the content based on media format. Questions at the end of each chapter will help you introduce media literacy in your home or classroom. Media literacy might not *save* the world, but it sure can *improve* the world by helping us see how we consume information, perceive others, learn, view the world, and even vote.

Let's get started.

Why Promote Media Literacy?

"For me, as a consumer of media, as well as an educator, media literacy education involves taking back our inherent rights of freedom of thought from the outlets that attempt to monitor, persuade, and condition our minds." —*Tim Kohler, high school English teacher and former student*

Media Literacy at Home:

- Are you an active or passive media consumer? What difference does it make?
- In what ways do the media influence your life or your family?
- Are there media productions that you and your family enjoy together?

Media Literacy in the Classroom:

- How do students define media?
- Are students aware of how much media they consume? Could they chart it?
- In what ways do your students feel that the media affect them?

QR CODES

**PDF: Why Media
Literacy Is Important**

**TED Talk on Media Literacy
for Critical Thinking**

**PDF: Intro to
Media Literacy**

FOOTNOTES

---

[1] James E. Short, "How Much Media? 2013 Report on American Consumers" (presentation, Institute for Communication Technology Management at the USC Marshall School of Business, Los Angeles, CA, October 2013).

[2] Nina Munk, "Culture Cops," *Forbes,* March 27, 1995, 43.

[3] Marjorie Ferguson, "Invisible Divides: Communication and Identity in Canada and the United States," *Journal of Communications,* 43, no. 2 (Spring 1993): 46.

[4] "The Core Principles of Media Literacy Education," *National Association for Media Literacy Education,* accessed June 13, 2015, http://namle.net/publications/core-principles/.

2

TELEVISION

FACTS TO REMEMBER:

- ☛ Everything on television is constructed to keep us watching.
- ☛ Heavy viewing of television can distort one's view of the world.
- ☛ Television's function is to deliver viewers to specific advertisers.
- ☛ Most channels are owned by a small number of huge media corporations.

Decades have passed since FCC Chairman Newton Minow declared television a "vast wasteland." At that time, television didn't have much competition for entertainment within the home. My students smirk when they learn I grew up watching only three channels—ABC, CBS, and NBC. Their television experience is of a dramatically different landscape, with hundreds of channels from which to choose. I wonder what Minow would say about the expansion of this "wasteland." Add to that plethora of stations the ability to watch programs *on demand*, and it's evident just how much the world of television has changed in even the past fifteen years. Students have a hard time imagining the *trial* of having to be in front of the television the minute a program broadcasts. It's increasingly common for streaming services on smartphones, computers, and tablets to deliver television content today. And thanks to TiVO and DVR technology, people rarely watch television programs when originally aired.

"Television is a medium of entertainment which permits millions of people to listen to the same joke at the same time, and yet remain lonesome." —T. S. Eliot

Changing with the Times

"Time shifting"—seeing *what* we want *when* we want—has led to a real revolution in immediacy. We are no longer held captive by the networks' programming schedules. "On-demand" technology provides an experience that is a far cry from when television began its prominence in the 1950s. At that time, the "Big Three" networks aimed for *broad*casting, meaning they tried to reach the broadest audience possible. Since these powerhouses had no competition for in-home entertainment, some programs achieved "seventy shares."

That incredible rating meant that *seventy percent* of the televisions turned on at a specific time were tuned into the same program.

"When you're young, you look at television and think there's a conspiracy. The networks have conspired to dumb us down. But when you get a little older, you realize that's not true. The networks are in business to give people exactly what they want." —Steve Jobs

A single company often sponsored a program. Can you imagine the *Camel News Caravan* airing today, with the anchor puffing on Camel cigarettes while he read the news? Variety shows like *The Ed Sullivan Show* and sketch comedy shows like *Your Show of Shows* created content to deliver the widest possible audience to advertisers. And audiences responded.

Drama programs told basic, one-plotline stories, and sitcoms represented the "ideal" American family. Remember how Lucy always schemed to be in Ricky's show on *I Love Lucy* and how Ricky always discouraged this? After all, Lucy was "only" a woman. It wasn't until later that television added meat to the menu by creating more complicated dramas and sitcoms that represented significant changes in our cultural landscape. With *Mary Tyler Moore*, for example, television followed society and let Mary get a job and remain single! Even the lyrics of the show's theme song its first season carried a banner for women at the time: *You might just make it on your own.*

It's interesting to contemplate what our grandparents might think about today's television shows—portraying sex without consequences, teenagers who talk with casual glibness, and very few nuclear families. But early television viewers might also have trouble keeping up with the numerous plotlines in shows today. The first time my parents watched *24*, my mother commented afterward she "didn't really get it." Later, I discovered that she had been working on a crossword puzzle during the show, something she had typically done while watching older, less complicated shows. Jack Bauer, however, was a more demanding subject.

More Stations, More Focused Markets

Cable and the VCR dramatically changed the landscape for the networks in the 1970s, freeing us from the schedule of the big three networks. If you're in your mid-forties, but, like me, are only twenty in your mind, you likely remember the day the cable box arrived. Suddenly, we had *more* channels, and channels from *other* cities—New York, Chicago, Atlanta! When I tell this story in class, I dance around excitedly, and my students look at me like I am nuts. (Actually, they look at me like that most of the time. But that's a story for another day.) And when I show them television listings from 1964 that stop at 2 a.m., they respond with, "What comes on after that?" They simply cannot grasp the concept of the striped test pattern or, worse, simple static remaining on the screen for hours.

Students today have grown up with hundreds of channels, and a majority of those national networks broadcast twenty-four hours a day. Technology makes it possible for them to watch what they want, when they want—a far cry from having to be home by 7 p.m. on a Thursday night to watch a single episode of *The Cosby Show* on NBC.

"If it weren't for electricity, we'd all be watching television by candlelight." —George Gobel

Television dramas today are more complicated as technology enables writers to incorporate serial-like aspects that weren't previously possible. If we miss an episode, scene, or piece of dialogue, we just rewind the DVR. Likewise, while you can't start watching *The Walking Dead* in season four and expect to understand what's going on, thanks to technology, you can stream previous seasons to catch up. In fact, streaming services allow you to binge on entire seasons of programs!

Kids don't notice this immediacy and technology; they're accustomed to watching TV programs whenever they want. In fact, most of them don't even watch shows on televisions. The click of a mouse instantly delivers content to their personal electronic device, leaving television networks in a quandary. They don't exist to provide programming. They exist to make money.

Learning History through TV Sitcoms

One can learn quite a bit about social history while watching TV sitcoms. Besides the changing role of women in America, sitcoms also reflected the dynamic definition of "family." In the early days of TV, a *family* consisted of married parents, children, and the white picket fence. Think *Father Knows Best*. But as the definition of family evolved in society, that evolution was reflected within television programming as well. Today, your co-workers or your friends could be family. What other social changes are currently being reflected in television sitcoms?

The major networks hit their first financial bump when the VCR and cable television arrived and upset their apple cart. But the most interesting turn of financial events came in 1981, when an upstart cable channel decided to target one specific market rather than attempt to reach the largest possible audience. Who can forget the music of that launched rocket and the flag that proudly proclaimed MTV's domination of the cable landscape? Not only did

MTV specifically target a coveted age group, forgoing all others, but its content consisted of videos created and *freely supplied* by record companies who wanted to sell albums. Pure genius! The rub for the networks, however, was MTV's impact on advertising revenue. Instead of paying huge fees to the broadcasting networks, advertisers flocked to MTV because it was *narrowcasting*. MTV didn't want everyone to watch—it wanted *teenagers* to watch. And although the audience numbers may have been smaller than that of the broadcast networks, advertisers spent their money with MTV because that specific audience was 100 percent desirable.

"Watching television is like taking black spray paint to your third eye." —Bill Hicks

MTV's choice to narrowcast led to a revolution in the cable industry. Today, few networks aim for a huge audience. Instead, networks like *Golf Channel*, *Travel Channel*, *The History Channel*, *HGTV*, and *Logo TV* aim for niches that appeal to specific advertisers. Smart advertisers buy time on these stations because they're guaranteed to reach their specific market.

From Super Expensive to Really Cheap

Television viewing has become an individualized experience. We have *our* shows and *our* channels that we watch when *we* want. Only on one day a year does everyone watch the same live event at the same time on the same channel: Super Bowl Sunday. The Super Bowl is the seminal television event of the year for Americans. Weeks before kick-off, the news publicizes how much companies are willing to pay for a thirty-second spot during the broadcast. Many people roll their eyes at the cost, but, considering the reach of these ads, it is worth every penny. And we *all* watch them *live!* Besides, what do people talk about the day after Super Bowl Sunday? Not the game. People talk about the commercials! The Super Bowl is the only time this number of people watch the same show on the same channel *live*. A few other events, such as presidential inaugurations or other breaking news, may be viewed by the masses in real-time, but those programs are offered on several channels at once and rarely include commercial interruptions. The Super Bowl is king.

> **"Most people gaze neither into the past nor the future; they explore neither truth nor lies. They gaze at the television."**
> **—Radiohead**

Television has evolved in other ways besides the storylines and the narrowcasting. In the 1990s, a new TV genre was born: the "reality" show. Known in the television industry as *unscripted programs*, our students and kids don't know a world without them. We could debate forever about how "real" these programs are, but their relevance isn't about whether or not they have a script or plan, rather it's about why we watch.

Reality shows are compelling to watch for several reasons. They present fame as something desirable and easy to attain—even without a noticeable skill or talent. Whether we are watching a cooking contest or someone scheming on *Survivor*, we watch vicariously, perhaps making us more accepting of a lack of privacy in our daily lives. But our reasons for watching reality TV run deeper than

"Most people buy the highest quality television sets, only to watch the lowest quality television shows." —Jarod Kintz

dreams of stardom. One of my students said she enjoyed the MTV program *Jersey Shore* because it made her feel like "less of a slut." Though her comment disturbed me, it made perfect sense. Who hasn't seen an episode of *Hoarders* and felt better about their own housecleaning? Who hasn't watched *Real Housewives of Atlanta* and suddenly realized their family and friends are relatively happy and functional? Sometimes, people watch television programs for emotional or intellectual reasons, but that's not why we watch reality shows. These unscripted programs are satisfying because, by giving us a peek into someone else's crazy life, our lives feel a little more exciting without the risk. As author Jennifer Pozner explains in her book, *Reality Bites Back: The Troubling Truth about Guilty Pleasure TV,* "We revel in the bizarre antics, pitiful tears, wild hookups, and self-loathing insecurities. We vicariously savor all the delicious melodrama of the high school cliques and office gossip with none of the guilt."[1]

It's true that reality shows dominate television because they get good ratings, but that's their main attraction to producers. Producers are attracted because reality shows are relatively cheap to produce. For example, during the final season of NBC's *Friends*, each of the six cast members was paid $1 million per episode—for an eighteen-episode season. Additional costs, including salaries for the show's scriptwriters, costume designers, and set directors, raised the production company's expenses. Compare that cost to what it takes to produce

ABC's *The Bachelor*, where hundreds of women audition to be on the show for free. The production company rents a fancy house in an exotic location, pays for the host's salary and, of course, the wine, trips, and roses. Even so, compared to a normal production's costs, reality shows are inexpensive. With *Survivor*, the producer doesn't even have to pay for a roof over the cast members' heads!

Constructed for Your Viewing Pleasure

When I tell people what I teach for a living, they usually assume I don't like TV. Oh sure, I went through that phase with my oldest child—thinking I'd never let him watch television. I later decided that taking a shower was a good thing, and mommy naps were even better. So we watched *Scooby-Doo*, *SpongeBob*, *The Powerpuff Girls* and the like. I spent a lot of time telling him, "Now remember, these are all make-believe. Nothing on television is real." And then baseball season started. We live in St. Louis, Missouri, where Major League Baseball is nearly a religion and Opening Day is a *high holy day*. Suddenly I had a problem. I had told my toddler that everything on TV was *fake*, but the Cardinals game was *real*. Teaching him about television wasn't going to be as easy as I had thought.

"An intellectual snob is someone who can listen to the *William Tell Overture* and not think of *The Lone Ranger*." —Dan Rather

It turns out that I had it all wrong. Instead of telling him everything on television was make-believe, I should have said, "Everything you see is created to be viewed in a certain way." To my college students

I say, "Everything in the media is a *construction.*" And this is especially obvious with television.

Television broadcasts are the culmination of a thousand decisions:

- What should the set look like?
- What are the characters like? What races or genders will they be? Will they have jobs? How will they dress? How will they speak to and treat one another?
- In what way will the show be edited? Will music, lighting, or camera angles be used to make us feel a certain way?
- What will the story demonstrate about how the world works? Will there be a lesson in the story?
- What is "normal" in this television world?

These questions also shape non-fiction and non-scripted programs. Music, editing, close-ups, and framing are all tools a television producer can use to elicit reactions whether the show is a news program or a Major League Baseball game. So, while it's incorrect to say everything on television is make-believe, it *is* correct to say everything on television is the result of many decisions. Everything on television is *constructed*, and these constructions lead to basic formulas and frameworks for television shows.

For example, talk shows all have similar sets and formulas. Sitcoms last thirty minutes and normally utilize three cameras, familiar settings, and a laugh track, whereas dramas typically last one hour and include more close-ups and chapter-like storylines. Reality shows include one-person "confessional" scenes where the person speaks directly to the camera. In many cases, the framework of the programs determines the content. Whether we realize it or not, our minds recognize these formulas very quickly.

"All television is educational television. The question is, what is it teaching?" —Nicholas Johnson

These formulas are ubiquitous in current programs, as well as in the classic, syndicated shows that programmers call "evergreens." An evergreen is a program, such as *The Andy Griffith Show, Seinfeld,* or *The Simpsons,* which had more than one hundred episodes and was eligible for off-network syndication. That means it was a program that originally aired on one network and its production company sells the reruns to other networks. These evergreens will be rerun in syndication as long as television is a business because it's much cheaper to buy programs produced by someone else than it is to produce them, especially if these shows will bring in decent ratings.

In the past few years, the framework and formulas of sitcoms have begun to evolve. Although the predictable storyline formula remains, use of the three-camera technique and, thankfully, the laugh track has declined. (Although I once had a student count the number of laugh track laughs in an episode of *The Big Bang Theory.* There were over sixty—in a program lasting only twenty-two minutes!) Producers call the laugh track "sweetened live studio audience recording." I call it "condescending" because its use implies viewers don't know when to laugh—that, on our own, we don't know what is funny. Writers should have more faith in their writing and in their viewers. That's why programs without laugh tracks, like *The Middle, Modern Family*, and *Parks and Recreation*, feel so refreshing. Bellwethers, like *Malcolm in the Middle* and *The Office*, are to thank for this evolution. Perhaps sitcoms are growing up.

Influencing Our Perceptions of Fame

As my son grew older and his younger brothers arrived, I noticed other television programs had matured as well. Fewer children's shows were animated, and many of these live-action productions featured teen and pre-teen actors whose characters were famous in some way. For example, *Hannah Montana, Victorious, Big Time Rush*, and *Austin & Ally* were well-known singers or members of rock bands. It struck me as odd. Why do these programs make fame look so attainable or even desirable? And, what's worse, why is "famous" the default position for many of these characters?

Anyone questioning the impact that television programming can have needs to look no further than Jake Halpern's book *Fame Junkies*. Halpern asked teenagers in Rochester, New York, several questions about their lives and their perceptions of fame. The girls surveyed said they'd rather have dinner with Jennifer Lopez than with Jesus Christ (17.4 percent to 16.8 percent). They also said they'd rather be the personal assistant to a celebrity than be the president of Harvard, a Navy SEAL, a United States Senator, or the CEO of a major corporation.[3]

Most telling, the teens Halpern interviewed who watch more television than their peers were more likely to perceive fame as something that would improve their lives. Perhaps the definition of "fame" has changed. Are the girls on *16 and Pregnant* famous? Is a teenager famous if he has ten thousand Instagram followers or has a hundred likes of a selfie posted on Facebook? What about students who post videos of their escapades on YouTube and receive thousands of views? Surely they feel some sort of "fame." Regardless of how fame is defined today, its influence in television is certainly worth analyzing.

The *Real* Reason Mass Media Exists

When journalists Bob Woodward and Carl Bernstein investigated the Watergate story during the Nixon Administration, they were told to follow the money—to trace its origins. The same practice is wise when analyzing television from a media literacy perspective. The purpose of mass media is not to educate, inform, or entertain. The purpose of mass media is to make money for its stockholders. And the financial stakes are staggering. For example, Viacom's revenue for 2014 was $13.78 billion. The Walt Disney Company's revenue for its media networks was $21.15 billion in 2014 (that number doesn't include its movies, theme parks, or consumer products).

Most people know commercials help pay for shows. What they don't consider is how the economics of television influence what they watch or how that content impacts their personal, cultural, and political beliefs.

Being aware of ownership and profits is very important when evaluating television from a media literacy perspective. Did you know that most Americans have over one hundred television channels, but those channels are typically owned by one of only six companies? General Electric, Time Warner, The Walt Disney Company, NewsCorp, Viacom, and CBS own seventy percent of the channels on television. The concentration of ownership and the large amounts of money involved make television station owners less likely to take risks with new programming. Media producers will stick to familiar formulas, genres, and stereotyping, and they may limit the diversity of voices. Stations will also avoid airing programs and viewpoints that might negatively affect the bottom line.

Center for Media Literacy's Core Questions:

The Center for Media Literacy in California has a great list of questions that provides a good starting point for any media literacy discussion.[2]

- Who created this message?

- What creative techniques are used to get my attention?

- How might different people understand this message differently from me?

- What lifestyles, values, and points of view are represented in, or omitted from, this message?

- Why is this message being sent?

The fact that television programming, with its huge cultural influence, is controlled by a small number of people and media companies is worth analysis.

Who Decides What You See?

Even if a program is highly regarded by the critics, a network will cancel it if the ratings are low. Measuring the success of a program with ratings, however, is problematic and archaic. The sample consists of a small number of households, and the figures do not indicate whether the ads running during a particular program are actually *watched*. How often do you walk away from the television during a commercial break or fast-forward through the ads altogether? The Nielsen Company, the primary organization responsible for the ratings figures, uses eye-tracking software to understand what people look at on a computer screen, although it is not being used—yet—to monitor whether a person is actually looking at the television screen during a commercial. Until then, the company determines ratings based on the number of televisions that are on and what's showing on them.

Ratings are the main benchmark that measures a television program's popularity. One ratings point usually equals about one million households, and a "share" represents the percentage of televisions tuned into a specific program during a specific period. In addition to determining programming, these figures help set network rates for potential advertisers: the higher the rating and share, the higher the price for a thirty-second commercial spot. Advertisers understand that high ratings don't guarantee that people are paying attention to their commercials. Add to this the increased use of streaming or recorded content, which means viewers can (and often do) skip commercials altogether, and it's easy to see how inaccurate a measure ratings can be.

As a result, many companies use product placement as an alternative to regular advertising. Placing a product within a program prevents it from falling victim to the DVR or Netflix. Notice how many episodes of *Modern Family* revolve around Costco, Target, or the iPad. *The Amazing Race* features products from Travelocity. During challenges on *Survivor*, the winning team might earn a cold

Mountain Dew. None of this is accidental. Advertisers *pay* to have their products included in the show. And although product placement is a less obvious form of commercial, it can more effectively influence behavior. Seeing a character we love using a new or interesting product convinces us that it must be good.

"Television! Teacher, mother, secret lover." —Homer Simpson

Remember, television programs are not created to deliver entertainment to the audience. They are created to deliver a specific audience to advertisers. That's why so many programs are aimed at the coveted eighteen-to-thirty-four age group—the ones with discretionary income still willing to try new things. Those of us in our forties are buying fun things like insurance and are terrified of upcoming college expenses, and senior citizens aren't likely to switch any brands or try new things. So very few programs are aimed at older audiences.

Television is a huge part of our culture and life. Because of television, we've attended World Series games, Olympic games, presidential debates, and countless special events. We've learned about people we'll never meet and places we'll never go. Television is truly a window to the world. But it's important to remember who controls what we see through that window. If a stranger were allowed to come into your home and lecture your family about life, relationships, work, sex, and materialism without having your best interest at heart, would you allow it? Probably not. Yet the television is the centerpiece of most American family rooms. Let's start asking some questions about that stranger.

> **"Television is the most powerful thing that has ever been invented."**
> **—Ozzy Osbourne**

Co-Watching

Thousands of research studies have examined the television's effects on its viewers. Many researchers claim a link exists between viewing violence and being violent or viewing sexual activity and becoming sexually active at an earlier age. One of the most interesting studies I've seen, however, was conducted by Nicole Martins, who reviewed the substantial amount of teasing, sarcastic remarks, insults, eye-rolling, and name-calling in the top shows aimed at children ages two to eleven. In her research report "Mean on the Screen," she notes. "Compared to the portrayals of physical aggression, social aggression was more likely to be enacted by an attractive perpetrator, to be featured in a humorous context, and neither rewarded or punished." We know that children learn from what they see. If children can learn how to read by watching shows like Sesame Street, is it far-fetched to think they can also learn to be rude by watching television?

Rude behavior is not limited to shows for children. Consider Friends, The Big Bang Theory, or How I Met Your Mother, where many of the jokes are made at the expense of other characters. The insults are clever, glib, quick—and entertaining. This entertainment is not teaching us empathy or compassion. It's modeling behavior that for many children would involve a punishment.[4]

Many research studies have shown that "co-watching" a television program with a child is the first step to media literacy. Co-watching provides a great opportunity for you to ask questions about what they're seeing and, most importantly, what they think about what they're seeing. Sometimes when my family is watching a program together and I make an observation or ask a question, one of my sons will ask "Gee, Mom, can't we just watch a show without you analyzing it all the time?"

Co-watching a program with a child or student can be as easy as asking questions such as:

- "Why do you think that character just did that?"
- "What would *you* do in that situation?"
- "Is this something that would ever happen in real life? Why or why not?"
- "What is it about this program that you like?"
- "How does this program make you feel?"
- "Do you feel represented in this program?"

Why Promote Media Literacy?

"Everyone who consumes media should be aware of it, starting from an early age and continuing into adulthood. Everyone should understand that what we see is not always what we get. Companies are always trying to sell something even when their ads do not seem like it, and what we see and hear is not always truth. Ads are created based off of consumer interest, and consumer interest is generated through media. Thus, they rely on us just as much as we rely on them. In essence, we create the media that we see. The goal of media literacy is to understand what we have created."
–Ashley Cramer, former student

Media Literacy at Home:

- How do our favorite shows define us or our family?
- Is television the default activity in our home? Why or why not?
- Does our family have restrictions on TV viewing?
- What role models do we find on TV?

Media Literacy in the Classroom:

- Analyze the number of ads within a media message.
- Investigate how certain stereotypes are portrayed on TV.
- Evaluate "reality shows" with actual reality. How are they different?
- Have students critique the lives of kids portrayed on TV compared to their own.
- What can we learn about history by watching old TV shows?
- How much does a typical TV commercial cost? Why are there differences in ad costs?

QR CODES

Like any media clip, these should be viewed *before* showing to any students or kids. Some of them have a bit of vulgar language, but what they *show* is so fantastic that I am including them anyway.

**Video:
"How to
Recognize Reality
Show Editing Tricks"
(irreverent language)**

**Website:
The MediaSmarts
Television Page**

**Website:
Critical Viewing Skills
and Television**

**Video:
"History of TV: TV 101"**

**Video:
"Reality Show Editing"
(irreverent language)**

**Website:
Making TV Time Count**

FOOTNOTES

[1] Jennifer L. Pozner, *Reality Bites Back: The Troubling Truth about Guilty Pleasure TV* (Berkeley: Seal Press, 2010), 16.

[2] "CML's Five Key Questions," *Center for Media Literacy*, accessed on June 13, 2015, http://www.medialit.org/sites/default/files/14A_CCKQposter.pdf.

[3] Jake Halpern, *Fame Junkies: The Hidden Truths behind America's Favorite Addiction* (New York: Houghton Mifflin, 2007), xvi.

[4] Martins, Nicole and Barbara Wilson, "Mean on the Screen: Social Aggression in Programs Popular with Children." *Journal of Communication* 62, no. 6, (2012).

3

MUSIC AND THE RADIO

FACTS TO REMEMBER:

☛ Music can affect our emotions more than any other medium.

☛ Music distribution is basically controlled by Apple's iTunes.

☛ Only three companies own most of the major record labels.

☛ Radio is usually a secondary activity.

☛ News and talk radio are the highest-rated formats.

Nothing can change our mood or evoke memories as quickly as music. Tim Westergren, creator of the music streaming site Pandora, says, "Music can emotionally and spiritually transport us through our memories, which are a very powerful part of who we are." He's right! A song can send us back to childhood, make us feel happy or, as with Phil Collins' 1984 hit "Against All Odds," even remind us of a horribly dramatic high school break-up. We listen to music communally and individually in times of sadness, worship, or celebration. Sometimes we listen just for fun. Because it can affect us emotionally and since Americans tune in, on average, four hours a day, music and the way we listen to it deserves some analysis.[1]

In the Beginning...

Thanks to technology, we can hear any song we want with the tap of a finger. But radio didn't start out that way. As we analyze the impact of this medium on society today, it's important to understand its history. The next generation needs to be aware of what the enormous technological changes must have meant for its grandparents and great-grandparents.

"To a medieval peasant, a radio would have seemed like a miracle." —Richard Dawkins

Joking with my students, I've often said that Thomas Edison is a safe guess to any question about who invented almost any media product. Edison, the "Wizard of Menlo Park," certainly played a role in the development of recorded music. In 1877, he developed a recording device that played back voices and called it a *phonograph*, meaning sound (*phono*) and far away (*graph*).

In the late 1880s, German-born Emile Berliner went a step further and created a way to record sounds onto flat metal discs. These were the first master recordings that could be played on gramophones, the classic old-style record player with the attached, horn-shaped speaker. The gramophone was used to record French folk songs as early as 1900.

"The radio craze...will soon fade."
—Thomas Edison, 1922

Berliner's flat disc resembles a thick, silver, earlier version of the vinyl LP (record), which sends us down the family tree of recorded music: LP to magnetic tape reel-to-reel to 8-track tape to the cassette to the CD and, finally, to the music product that you can't actually touch—the MP3 file. What students don't appreciate now is the immediacy and availability of music. To them, the idea of fast-forwarding a cassette to get to a specific song seems ludicrous. Our kids have never had to wait for their favorite song. With the press of a button, they can hear whatever they want, whenever they want. Each new release of a music delivery system felt like a glimpse into the future. My students giggle when I tell them how a broken cassette could be fixed by pulling the magnetic tape out, splicing it, and rolling it back into the plastic case with the end of a pencil. And what person over forty doesn't remember the first CD he purchased? (Mine was U2's *War* in 1988.)

The music industry grew up alongside the radio industry that took hold of American culture after Guglielmo Marconi's invention of the "wireless telegraph." While history credits Marconi with the invention of the radio, he merely considered it a way to transmit

Morse code without wires. Lee de Forest conceived the idea of using the radio to transmit music and voice to a *large* audience.

Bringing Entertainment Home

Radios helped create the music industry of the mid-twentieth century. Can you imagine what it must have been like to have a radio in your home for the first time? Some people were initially frightened to hear voices in the house when no one else was home. But any fear was soon replaced with the novel thrill of being entertained at home. Prior to the creation of the radio, to see or hear a dramatic presentation, you had to go to the theater. Suddenly, this new machine allowed people to sit in the comfort of their homes and listen to the radio. *Sit and listen to the radio.* Today, listening to the radio, or to music in general, is considered a *secondary media activity*—something we typically do while we are studying, working, or driving. But in the mid-1900s, listening to the radio made for great entertainment.

"We're not a service industry. We're a business." —Bill Lueth, KDFC Program Director

From a media literacy standpoint, one entertainment event is particularly noteworthy: *The War of the Worlds* radio broadcast by Orson Welles in October of 1938. Welles performed a dramatic interpretation of the H.G. Wells story, presenting it as news bulletins and broadcast without commercial breaks, which added to the realism. Someone tuning into the program while it was in progress had missed the disclaimer that it was actually just a dramatic interpretation of the story. While the extent of the hysteria caused by the broadcast is still disputed, it's safe to say this was the first time the public had been duped by electronic mass media. The misinterpretation and its aftermath even made the front page of *The New York Times* the following day. Legend surrounding this story suggests the term "tin foil hats" originated on this night from people attempting to protect their brains from the laser beams of the invading Martians.

Students laugh at such stories now, giggling at the unsophisticated listeners who believed and trusted everything that came across the radio. Thankfully, listeners today are a bit more skeptical. *The War of the Worlds* story is one that will forever be told in media history classes as an example of a simpler time and media's power to influence public perceptions and behavior.

How Economics Shape the Radio and Music Industries

The radio industry and music industry may have grown up together, but technology has essentially split them.

Radio

Radio stations earn money the same way that television stations do—by selling advertising time. The price of an ad slot depends on when the commercial will air (morning and afternoon drive time segments are typically the most expensive) and how many people listen to the station. Ratings are put together several times a year, and ad salespeople use them to boost ad sales and prices. By selecting a station or time slot with a particular demographic, advertisers can use radio to target a specific audience.

Asking students which radio commercials they hate is fun because nearly every student has an ad they say drives them crazy. Ironically, the annoying commercial is the one they remember. So, by definition, it is a *good* ad.

"The radio of my youth is now a quaint memory replaced with hard drives." —Phil Donahue

Sadly, the disc jockey is no longer a huge part of the radio or music industry either. Stations lean now toward syndicated programming to lower costs and increase ratings. These programs are set in one city but played in hundreds, and purchasing these programs can actually be cheaper for a radio station than producing a local show of its own. Even the humans who do sit behind microphones at most stations do not have music control. Programming directors, who work for the large corporation that owns the station, select the music in advance. The disc jockey might provide a human voice for the station, but any choices made by the DJ are a thing of the past.

Radio personalities still exist, however, and in many cases, "para-social relationships" are formed. Listeners feel like they *know* the radio personalities. The personalities don't know us, but we know *them*. Once at a large gathering, I recognized my favorite radio personality who was standing behind me—purely by his voice. After I mustered up enough courage, I turned around, introduced myself and said, "You have no idea how much time we spend together." Not the best way to introduce oneself. I skulked away after that, amused that I'd been personally affected by the very thing I teach.

Music

Although the radio industry is still significant (radio reaches nine-ty-three percent of Americans twelve and older[2]), it is no longer the engine that fuels the music industry. We now listen, stream, and buy music online. Our music selections are more individualized than ever, meaning we rarely listen to music we did not choose ourselves. With portable music libraries and devices, we can customize our music selections at the press of a button to fit our taste and mood. De Forest may have considered radio a "from one to many" type of communication, but with technology, that communication has evolved to be more like "one to one." Our music collections are as unique as our fingerprints.

Changes in the music industry go much deeper than simply the technology. Like television, the industry is now dominated by very few players. Universal Music Group, a division of the French media conglomerate Vivendi, controls forty percent of the world's commercial music library. These artists include U2, The Beatles, and The Beach Boys—artists who have staying power when it comes to broadcast rights.

"Research rarely gives recognition to originality. It recognizes what's familiar." —Warren Littlefield, NBC

Warner and Sony, the other two major players in the music industry, control nearly the rest of the worldwide music market. So we're looking at essentially only three music companies, all part of huge corporations that typically aren't interested in artistic creativity unless it will guarantee profits.

That focus on profits brings us to a standard criticism of the music industry: homogenization, the idea that most commercial music sounds eerily similar. This is not by accident. Why sign a recording deal to an artist who might not make a profit? Companies are more likely to sign artists with a sound similar to that which has already proven commercially successful. Why would music producers take risks? After all, these companies are not in the entertainment business; they're in the profit-making business.

"Radio is the theatre of the mind. Television is the theatre for the mindless." —Steve Allen

Which company is making the most profit in the music business? Surprisingly, it's not a music company at all. Apple generated $4.5 billion in revenue from iTunes alone, just in the second quarter of 2014. While Warner and Sony were busy suing the song-sharing site Napster, Apple developed a new, legal, and profit-based music delivery system—and never looked back. Analysts of the music industry say that Apple now controls worldwide music distribution.

Also fascinating is how television and MTV have played a role in the music industry. Television moved us from a literate society to more of a visual society. We are image-based. So how does the physical attractiveness of a music artist affect his potential for success, if at all? My students don't believe me when I tell them that my favorite band in childhood—The Police—was my favorite before I even knew what they looked like. Like any other retail product, musicians today are perfectly packaged for presentation on YouTube and television.

Social Impact of Music

I'm a music enthusiast and typically have music playing, in one form or another, every waking moment. When my kids were little, I'd hurry to turn the volume down before they heard any "bad words." I continued this until my oldest said, "Mom, it's okay. We ride the bus to public school."

My concern then turned to the actual content of the lyrics. How was I supposed to protect my kids from hearing people they admire sing about drugs and, my least favorite, using the word "party" as a *verb*? Turns out that my kids, and many of my students as well, don't pay much attention to the lyrics. If they *do* pay attention, they often make fun of how silly they are. That's not to say lyrics never influence listeners, but to assume that all lyrics have negative effects might be a stretch.

"Music washes away from the soul the dust of everyday life." —Berthold Auerbach

Much has been written about objectionable lyrics within pop music. When this topic comes up in class, it's obvious that everyone has a different definition of "objectionable." The First Amendment allows one to oppose objectionable lyrics but not outlaw them, which is why media literacy is so important. We can't change the message or the sender, but we can educate the receiver.

One compelling issue for discussion is the presence of specific products mentioned within songs. In the last ten years, the mention of specific alcohol brands within songs has increased twenty-one percent. If a teenager listens to three hours of music daily, she hears three thousand alcohol references within song lyrics annually, even though it is illegal to advertise alcohol to minors. Does this count as advertising? When Jay Z buys a champagne company and then includes those bottles in all of his music videos, does the video become an alcohol commercial? When parents and teachers tell kids that alcohol can be harmful, how are pro-alcohol messages from pop stars processed by those kids?

"Sometimes I feel like rap music might be the way to end racism." —Eminem

Thousands of studies examine the role of women in music videos. Countless examples can be found of scantily clad women acting as mere decorations for the male vocalist. However, music videos aren't the sole culprit here; there's more than enough misogyny to go around in the electronic mass media. As with media formats, however, the way the music industry portrays women has the potential to affect the culture's view of how women should look and behave.

When the average American spends more than ten hours a day with mass media, some influence is all but guaranteed. But what if all that exposure is a good thing? Could song lyrics bring about social change? Just as Harriet Beecher Stowe's *Uncle Tom's Cabin* exposed much of the country to the evils of slavery, perhaps song lyrics can also teach us about social issues. Think of the classic protest songs from the 1960s or hip-hop songs from the 1990s about social justice. Song lyrics can raise society's consciousness of an issue much better than any television news interview could do.

Songs and song lyrics can raise more than consciousness—they can raise money, too. The 1985 all-star anthem "We Are the World" raised over $60 million to fight hunger in Africa.[3] That a recording did this—and not a film or television program—demonstrates how powerfully music can affect our emotions and call us to action.

What's Next for Music Media?

When you love something, it's only natural to share it. So it's no surprise that the public's desire to watch and share music products online—especially music videos—has created some headaches for music labels as well as artists. The band OK Go, for example, has created some incredibly popular music videos. These creative and interesting videos have been shared and viewed millions of times. You'd think their record label would consider this a good thing, right? Wrong.

"If you believe I am a cop killer, then you believe David Bowie is an astronaut." —Ice T

OK Go's label, EMI, effectively blocked their YouTube videos from being embedded in other sites like blogs, news sites, or articles since it only received royalties from YouTube views. When the block went into effect, OK Go's video viewership dropped ninety percent. Ironic, since EMI could have considered the massive embedding of the videos to be free advertising for the band. Since then, OK Go has dropped EMI as their record label.

The next big issue for the music industry will be how it plans for and reacts to the changing delivery system of streaming music versus purchased music. Is music a product—or a service? Websites can now personalize playlists based on the "genetic code" of a song so that you never have to listen to a song you won't enjoy. How will the music industry respond when we can simply use online streaming services to enjoy their products? We no longer buy albums or compact discs. Has the time come when we no longer have to buy MP3 files as well? Enough fodder exists here for loads of media literacy discussion and exercises. Let's get busy.

Why Promote Media Literacy?

"Media literacy is critical to the education of our children because it allows them to engage productively with the ocean of information that surrounds them. Increasingly, our world has become less and less about what a person can recite or regurgitate. Our children will need to be equipped not only to sift through and identify valid sources but also to make connections among what they find and, ultimately, act using the connections they made in that data soup. Media literacy is the building block that all of those skills rest upon."
–*Tyann Cherry, associate director of online programs at Southern Illinois University Edwardsville*

Media Literacy at Home:

- Why do we prefer certain styles of music over others?

- What influences our music taste?

- Which songs evoke specific memories for you?

Media Literacy in the Classroom:

- How do songs from particular time periods differ?

- In what ways are cultural changes represented in music?

- How are song lyrics poetry? Which lyrics promote social change?

- Can music have a physiological effect on us?

QR CODES

**Website: Music Industry's
99 Problems**

**Website: History of
the Music Video**

**TED Talk: The Four Ways
that Sound Affects Us**

**Video: War of the Worlds
Entire Radio Program**

FOOTNOTES

[1] "Edison Research Conducts First Ever Share of Ear™ Measurement for All Forms of Online and Offline Audio," *Edison Research*, accessed June 13, 2015, http://www.edisonresearch.com/edison-research-conducts-first-ever-share-of-ear-measurement-for-all-forms-of-online-and-offline-audio/.

[2] "Key Indicators in Media & News," *Pew Research Center Journalism and Media*, accessed June 13, 2015, http://www.journalism.org/2014/03/26/state-of-the-news-media-2014-key-indicators-in-media-and-news/.

[3] Roger Catlin, "USA for Africa: Five Years, $106 Million," *The Sun Sentinel* (Fort Lauderdale), April 15, 1990.

4

FILM

FACTS TO REMEMBER:

☞ Hollywood avoids risk and, therefore, sticks with proven formulas.

☞ Nearly eighty percent of the films released by Hollywood are financial failures.

☞ Blockbusters are how the major studios earn back that money.

☞ Movie ratings are arbitrary and done voluntarily.

What is your favorite movie? If you had to, could you pick just one? Or do you love entire genres? One of the reasons our favorite movies are listed on our social media profiles and make such great conversation starters is because, more than any other medium, our film choices reveal a lot about our personalities.

A certain magic happens when we go to the movies. We engage in the "willing suspension of disbelief." We know Middle Earth and the Death Star don't actually exist, but we willingly go there anyway. We play along with the movie producers and let them take us places, which gives the movie maker an unprecedented amount of power. But even as we grip the edge of our seat during a thriller or hold hands during a romantic comedy, as with other media, we have to take responsibility for understanding how and why films are crafted and produced.

"Everything I learned, I learned from the movies." —Audrey Hepburn

Even though movies are increasingly purchased or streamed for home entertainment, the movie industry itself still plays an enormous role in our culture and economy. The six major movie studios showed a profit of $6.3 billion in 2013 alone. Movie releases are *events,* unrivaled by any other media, except perhaps television on Super Bowl Sunday. Of course, movies didn't always hold so much appeal.

From Moving Pictures to Blockbuster Events

Moviegoers today would likely find Hollywood's earliest films unwatchable. The scenes are *long,* and special effects were created by "crazy" techniques like editing, rather than CGI. If you're skeptical, check out *The Great Train Robbery* on YouTube and attempt to stay awake!

Remember my tip about Thomas Edison being a safe guess for questions related to media invention? He wrote in 1888, "I am experimenting upon an instrument which will do for the eye what the radio does for the ear." The first step was the kinetoscope, a peephole-type viewer for moving pictures. But the kinetoscope only allowed one person to watch at a time. Not until the Lumière brothers developed a projection system in 1895 could movies be watched by more than one person at a time.

The Lumière brothers also developed a special camera that could capture moving pictures, and they used it to film the arrival of a train at the station in La Ciotat, France. The fifty-second clip captured a long, medium, and close–up shot of a train pulling into the station. Legend says, when the Lumière brothers showed this clip for the first time, several audience members ran screaming to the back of the theater in fear of the oncoming train. They had never seen a realistic moving picture like this! We laugh at this sort of reaction now, but people in the 1890s were *shocked* to see a picture come to life like this.

"The length of a film should be directly related to the endurance of the human bladder."
—Alfred Hitchcock

As technology continued to improve, the novelty of moving pictures attracted audiences. By 1909, more than ten thousand nickelodeons—small storefront theaters—had popped up across America. Commonly referred to as "democracy's theater," they were cheap enough for everyone to afford and these silent films' subtitles even helped many new immigrants improve their

English skills. Initially, piano players and basic sound effects accompanied silent films. By the 1920s, opulent movie palaces were being built. Organists played along enormous screens in these huge, ornate cinemas. What an experience that must have been!

"All you need to make a good movie is a girl and a gun." —Jean-Luc Godard

Before World War I, Europe produced as many films as Hollywood. The war took a toll on Europe's economy and infrastructure as Hollywood took sole possession of first place. Although movies are made all over the world today, Hollywood remains the leader.

The technological advances of the last few decades have done more for the film industry than simply making special effects easier. New technologies have also democratized film creation. With a phone, a video editing app, and some music, anyone can practice film production. The next Stephen Spielberg might currently have his or her own YouTube channel.

Show Me the Money!

Just as radio did, Hollywood struggled when television came along. Since people could be entertained in their homes for the first time, movie revenues decreased. To counteract the effect of television, the movie industry tackled topics that television wouldn't touch in the 1940s and 50s: adultery, child sexuality, war, and violence. Movies, like television, follow an easily identifiable framework. Genres—western, romantic comedy, science fiction, or fantasy—are used in movies and television because viewers are accustomed to particular storylines and myths within our culture.

Since the movie industry is controlled by a very small number of companies, much like television and music, we need to remember that profit is more important to them than artistic creativity. Genres are predictable, which allow movie producers to avoid financial risks. They know that superhero flicks and science fiction or fantasy adventures consistently land among the highest-grossing domestic films. Typically part of a franchise or based on books or comic book characters, these high-intensity films deliver the box office results producers want. In contrast, a dialogue-driven drama set in the Midwest probably won't do as well domestically—and may not even make it to the overseas markets. An action thriller set in a fantasy world can translate very well into other cultures. After all, car chases and explosions are the same in every language!

"Good movies make you care, make you believe in possibilities again." —Pauline Kael

Would you be surprised to know that over eighty percent of the films produced by Hollywood are considered financial losses because they generate less money than they cost to produce? So how does Hollywood make money? Film profits are driven by "tent pole" projects—commonly called blockbusters—so named because they hold up the rest of the industry. Students can usually identify the traits of a modern blockbuster: huge budget, loads of special effects, and retail merchandise. Successful blockbusters generate reboots years later. Usually released in the summer and promoted like crazy, the profits from a blockbuster enable a studio to make its other movies. And since companies are risk averse, if a blockbuster makes a lot of money, its sequel is probably in the works before opening weekend has concluded.

Like television, Hollywood also makes a significant amount of money with product placement. We can find ourselves in the middle of a two-hour commercial when we actually thought we were going to a movie! Product placement in film is a brilliant form of advertising. Who can forget Wilson, the volleyball friend of Tom Hanks' character in *Cast Away* or James Bond's favorite brand of car? There are agencies in Hollywood whose sole purpose is to place brands within movies under production. Remember that nothing shows up in a movie accidentally.

"It's not what a movie is about, it's how it is about it." —Roger Ebert

The movie business generates enormous amounts of money, way beyond ticket sales. DVD sales, streaming rights, international box office sales, and merchandise are all involved as well. Because of this, marketing campaigns for movies can be intense. The main movie studios—Disney, Paramount, Warner Brothers, and 20th Century Fox—are all owned by huge multinational media corporations. These companies also own television networks, television production companies, magazine publishers, radio stations, and newspapers. Using all of their resources to advertise a tent pole film is extremely easy and convenient. This is why you will see the stars of the next blockbuster film on the cover of magazines, on talk shows, radio interviews, and in newspaper articles. I'll say it again: nothing is accidental. Movies are a money game and the house stacks the deck in its favor.

The Next Time You Go to the Movies...

Because movies offer a different and sometimes longer experience than other media, they provide an opportunity to fully evaluate the production values that help us identify movie genres. And once we begin to notice how films use production values to tell a story, it's nearly impossible to *stop* noticing. The next time you watch a movie, pay attention to the following elements:

- How does music help tell the story?

- Does lighting or camera angles make you feel certain ways about characters?

- What about the script? Is the dialogue believable?

- How does editing help create tension?

- Does color play a special role in telling the story?

- How important are special effects in the storytelling?

What's It Rated? (And Why?)

How many times have you been at a movie with your child and cringed when a character said a word you really didn't want your little one to hear? Or chosen film for your students to watch, only to realize *as you were watching it with them* that the content wasn't suitable for all audiences? The content in movies has always generated great interest. Some critics claim movies are too violent or contain too much sex. Study after study attempts to link violent media consumption with violent behavior.

The movie rating system resulted from studies done in the 1920s and 30s by the Payne Foundation, a private fund which set out to determine how regular movie attendance affected children. The results revealed that heavy movie-watchers experienced fear and anxiety and suffered from sleep problems. The research had problems, of course, since the medium was still relatively new and the sample was small, but the results were enough to encourage the industry to start voluntarily labeling movies that might not be appropriate for younger viewers. So the rating system essentially protects the film industry itself by shifting responsibility from the studio to the viewers.

> **"Never compare your love story to the ones in the movies. They are written by script writers."**
> **—Efren Peñaflorida, Jr.**

Movie ratings have evolved over the years, with the current ratings appearing in 1968 and the addition of PG-13 in 1984. In 1990, the Motion Picture Association of America started listing the reasons for a given rating. For example, smoking was added as a ratings-based content item in 2007. Crude humor, thematic elements, intense violence, sexuality, nudity, drug use, and language are just a few warnings that help potential viewers know if the movie is one they want to watch.

What Do We Learn from Movies?

We learn from movies what we learn from most mass media. We learn what behavior is accepted and normalized. We might learn that violence is an easy way to settle disputes or that there are no repercussions to sexual activity. But we might also learn to be inspired, motivated, or called to action.

Many of my college students seem to learn about romance from the movies. In the movies, the romance comes quickly, suffers a setback, and then the couple reunites at the end to "live happily ever after." Romantic comedies follow a simple and familiar formula. But do they give us an unrealistic view of romance, relationships, and the opposite sex? Is it possible to watch these films and *not* have an idealized view of love?

Surprisingly, my male students get the most upset about the way love and romance are depicted in movies. They claim that films set up unrealistic standards for men and that they can't compete with the image portrayed in the movies. For example, one of my students a few years ago did a presentation on how the film *The Notebook* ruined his own relationship. Apparently, his girlfriend broke up because he "wasn't as romantic as Noah in the movie."

We can enjoy movies as responsible entertainment simply by being aware that films, even those "based on a real-life story," are fiction. They're created to entertain *and* to entice us to spend. Movies are big business. They're a part of American culture, and they affect us. So instead of simply showing and watching them, let's study and analyze them.

Why Promote Media Literacy?

"Being media literate changes my entire thought process when watching a film. I am constantly looking for the strategies and techniques the director uses to grab and keep my attention. I like to look for how color is being used because I know it is being used to subtly impact my emotion. I also find it interesting to hear how music and dialogue are leveraged to tell the story. The music always seems to match the pace and flow of a scene. In other words, I'm constantly aware that my choices and emotions are being manipulated." –*Don Goble, Ladue School District, St. Louis, Missouri*

Media Literacy at Home:

- What do our favorite movies say about us?

- When has a movie affected us emotionally?

- Notice how movie trailers make every movie look fantastic? How and why do they do that?

- Are there parts of movies that aren't realistic? Which ones?

Media Literacy in the Classroom:

- How does music affect the mood of a film?

- Does the movie rating system need improvement? Why or why not?

- Which movie characters represent you?

- Are there movies that distort history? If so, why do they?

QR CODES

Video: Intro to Film Techniques and Terms

Video: Famous *Star Wars* Scene without Music

Gallery: Film Poster Clichés

Video: How Music Can Change a Film

Website: Daily, Weekly, Yearly, and All-Time Box Office Figures

Website: Understanding Film Ratings

Story: What Your Favorite Movie Says about You

Power of Editing and Music: *Frozen* as a Horror Film

FOOTNOTES

1 Samuel Taylor Coleridge, *Biographia Literaria* (London: n.p., 1817), Chapter XIV.

2 "Worldwide Grosses #1-100," *Box Office Mojo,* accessed June 13, 2015, http://www.boxofficemojo.com/alltime/world/.

3 "Why Do All Hollywood Movies Lose Money?" *Priceonomics*, accessed June 13, 2015, http://priceonomics.com/why-do-all-hollywood-movies-lose-money/.

5
NEWS

FACTS TO REMEMBER:

☞ A news product is produced to make money, not inform.

☞ News is primarily visual; importance is given to stories with video.

☞ Technology has made news instant.

☞ News outlets race to be first, rather than correct.

Media literacy discussions aren't complete without talking about the news. Twenty-four hours a day, a constant flow of information streams to our computers, televisions, smartphones, tablets, and radios. News comes immediately and without context, and frames the world for us. The question is: Are we better informed than we were before the mass media existed? Perhaps we need to reevaluate what being "informed" means. Without question, media literacy is both essential and extremely relevant to our everyday lives when it comes to news.

Sparking Revolutions

News has been around forever—from stone carvings to newspapers, to today's digital, immediate, and visual reports. The effects of this evolution deserve analysis, especially since "...the news has the ability to define the agenda, by leading the attention of an audience to what it believes to be the issues of importance."[1]

The *Boston News-Letter* was the first major newspaper in the American colonies, carrying old news from England and, of course, all the local illnesses and floggings. While my students and I roll our eyes at the stories that were deemed most important to cover, we then admit the first page we check when we read the campus newspaper is the *crime* section. Perhaps humanity's tastes in "news" haven't evolved after all!

Historians claim that Ben Franklin's *Pennsylvania Gazette* was the best colonial paper. One thing's for sure: Franklin was savvy enough to sell advertising space in his paper. His revenue-generating idea still influences today's news media, nearly three hundred years later.

During colonial times, presses were busy printing Thomas Paine's *Common Sense* and the weekly *Boston Gazette*. In fact, historian Eric Burns credits newspapers with starting, covering, and winning the Revolutionary War.

It was newspapers who kept the colonies informed of the progress of the fighting in a way that letters and patterers could not have done, and, in the process, united the colonies in a way that was beyond the ability of the jerry-built wartime government.[2]

Low literacy rates and a lack of infrastructure to print and deliver large quantities kept newspaper circulation relatively small in the 1770s and 1780s. Over time, as the literacy rate improved and production costs fell, newspaper publishing and readership expanded. This increased interest in news in the early 1800s ushered in the "penny paper" phase, in which serialized stories, sensationalism, and celebrity news came into fashion.

"Sometimes negative news does come out, but it is often exaggerated and manipulated to spread scandal." —Pope Francis

The Civil War period saw the birth of the wire service. Transmitting news by telegraph allowed six newspapers in New York to pool their resources, send only one reporter to certain battles, and then share the story. The Associated Press (AP) was born! Today, more than 1,400 American newspapers use the AP service to access national and international news stories. Similar to the idea of syndicated programming on radio and television stations, using AP stories and photos is much less expensive than sending reporters on location. The downside of this efficient, cost-effective service is that, because so many papers heavily rely on the AP, much of today's news comes from a single, original source.

The success of penny papers like *The New York Sun* brought a shift in the newspaper industry's focus from "hard" news, which concentrated on facts, to "soft" news, like feature stories. Around this time, Joseph Pulitzer started the *St. Louis Post-Dispatch.* Pulitzer's new paper targeted women by featuring horoscopes, advice columns, and stories about fashion. Since women made most of the purchasing decisions, Pulitzer figured his advertising space would be more effective.

Transitioning to 24/7 News

Technology, concentration of ownership, and television worked together in the mid-twentieth century to forever change the concept of news. Initially, television networks aired news segments as a public service; they felt it was their duty to offer news programs in exchange for their license to operate on the public airwaves. News on television, at this point, was sporadic, shown throughout the day in five- and ten-minute intervals. Once network executives discovered that news programs could garner good ratings, they began to sell advertising time. In fact, NBC went one step further and let Camel cigarettes sponsor an entire news program called the *Camel News Caravan* where the newscaster sat at a desk and smoked—you guessed it—Camel cigarettes!

Television news became the fastest news delivery system, a concept that is hard for my students to understand. When I show them the black and white clip of Walter Cronkite announcing the death of President John Kennedy on November 22, 1963, they watch as Cronkite takes off his glasses and states that the President had died "…some thirty-eight minutes ago." Cronkite's announcement hangs in the air a bit, but within a few seconds, my students to start to ask, "Why did it take so long?" and, "What was everyone doing for those thirty-eight minutes?"

They are experiencing the "CNN Effect." With twenty-four-hour news, we are used to seeing news live and immediately. For example, when the second plane crashed into the South Tower of the World Trade Center in 2001, we saw it live—as it happened. Today's delivery systems have changed the idea of news as well as the way we process and experience it.

Cable TV stations changed the news landscape forever when they began offering twenty-four-hour news reports in the 1990s. Instead of snippets of news throughout the day, where editors had to determine what was important enough to mention, channels now have twenty-four hours a day, seven days a week to cover the issues of the day. I've come to the conclusion that the change didn't necessarily improve news delivery. With so much time to fill, cable stations tend to turn to "talking heads," instead of actual reporters. They use opinions, conjecture, and repetition to turn minor stories into huge ordeals. I'm convinced if we had ten minutes of news a day—instead of 1,440—we'd be better informed.

"It's amazing that the amount of news that happens in the world every day always just exactly fits the newspaper."
—Jerry Seinfeld

Because news comes at us nonstop, we tend to hear a lot about things Walter Cronkite would never have considered "newsworthy." Celebrity marriages, celebrity divorces, murder trials happening on the other side of the country, never-ending weather reports, and live "team coverage" from a location where an event happened hours ago all provide fodder for the twenty-four-seven news cycle. How are we to discern what's significant when everything is treated as *breaking news*? Author and scholar Neil Postman predicted this "information glut" more than thirty years ago.

> We are a culture consuming itself with information, and many of us do not even wonder how to control the process. We proceed under the assumption that information is our friend, believing that cultures may suffer grievously from a lack of information, which, of course, they do. It is only now beginning to be understood that cultures may also suffer grievously from information glut, information without meaning, information without control mechanisms.[3]

Postman claimed that we would be so inundated with information that it would be impossible for us to determine what is valid, meaningful, or true. He also suggested the sheer amount of information would change what it meant to "be informed." This would explain why many of my students can name every single Kardashian, but not a single United States Senator.

A Picture's Worth 1,000 Words

The advent of television and cable made our news material much more visual than literary. Since content must be compatible with each media format, a newspaper story will be more word-based, while a television story will be more image-based. In fact, most television news programs refuse to cover a story without compelling visuals to accompany it. What does this mean? It means a late-night fire at an empty warehouse—ignored by a newspaper—may be the lead story on the television news if it includes visual coverage. And what difference does this make? We need to consider that our preferred format of news can influence what stories are included and omitted and why.

"People get confused and think there is no difference between news and entertainment. People who project themselves as journalists on television don't know the first thing about journalism. They are just there stirring up a hockey game." —Gary Ackerman

When consuming primarily visual news, we also need to realize that photos and video clips rarely tell the whole story. A news photo might be compelling, but it is only a short moment in time, rarely accompanied by a full story. Like Alain de Botton writes, "...pictures that make it into print are compressed, bland, repetitive, clichéd and sidelined, and are seen, unsurprisingly, as nothing more than blocks of color that can break up monochromatic runs of text."[4] In many cases, the photo itself acts as the story. Captions might attempt to explain or describe the photo, but their power is limited by space. The words chosen for the captions can also be biased or misleading. And did you know that many news photographs are altered? Technology makes it impossible for us to tell.

Video clips used in news may not be any more informative. Typically, they are simply intended to be a backdrop for the voice-over. However, researchers have determined that we are more likely to be drawn in by the visuals than by the words being spoken. So, even if the video isn't particularly engaging, we pay attention to the story it tells over and above any words that may be attached.

The need to evaluate the effects of visual media is simple: An image, be it a compelling news photo or disturbing video clip, is not only easily remembered but can also cause an emotional response. Upon seeing something upsetting, we might form a judgment on the situation without knowing the whole story—and we cannot depend on today's news media to ever tell us the whole story. Even if they attempt to, the story is quickly followed by another. With this quick succession of stories, Postman explained, "The newscaster means you have thought long enough on the previous matter… and that you must now give your attention to another news fragment or commercial."[5] The newscaster moves quickly from story to story to avoid upsetting viewers to the point they aren't interested in advertisers' products.

"Headlines, in a way, are what mislead you, because bad news is a headline and gradual improvement is not." —Bill Gates

Social *Proof?*

Since much news is transferred via social media today, traditional news outlets have to rush to compete. In their hurry, news outlets risk sending out information before it's been vetted for accuracy. Following breaking news stories via social media can be especially hazardous to one's critical thinking. Stories get retweeted or posted without much checking. A breaking story typically evolves over time, and time is the enemy of the current news business. Quick may not always be correct, but it is certainly preferred.

"Bad news travels at the speed of light; good news travels like molasses."
—Tracy Morgan

Critical consumption of news information has never been more important! I suggest to my students they have an "internal BS detector" activated at all times, regardless of the news source. As with music, television, and film, most news outlets, regardless of format, are owned by a very small number of large corporations, so profit is a major consideration. News programs and networks can charge more for advertising time if their ratings are high. To increase their ratings, they tell us stories we *want* to hear rather than ones we *need* to hear. News is becoming more like entertainment, and these news programs have a lot of competition for our attention. Additionally, in order to keep us watching, news producers are encouraged to sensationalize stories. We get hyperbole (*It's the storm of the century!*), drama (*Watch the team come from behind!*), and fear (*Your child might be the victim of an online predator!*). And the news industry preys on our short attention spans. Yesterday's headline is forgotten today, in an attempt to move us on to the "next big story." News outlets, like every other media source, exist not to inform or educate, but to keep us tuned in so we can be delivered to their advertisers.

The truth is, the *whole story* can never be told because that would take entirely too long. Our attention spans are too short. Newscasts give us a photo or video of explosions and riots in the crisis area and then shuffle our eyeballs along to the next story. We might learn a bit about some events happening in the world, but rarely are we told the historical context behind the events. We consider ourselves "informed" without actually knowing the meaning behind the story of the day.

"The one function that TV news performs very well is that, if there is not news, we give it to you with the same emphasis as if it were." —David Brinkley

Learning the meaning behind today's headlines is an easy task, but a time-consuming one. We have every news source and blog post available at our fingertips, if we care enough to look. I often encourage my students to check out international news sources to see different points of view as well, since many international news sources are not profit-based like ours and tend to go into deeper detail. It may take time and effort, but it's worth it to those who are interested in the meanings behind the headlines.

News Channels Are NOT Nonprofits

Staggering amounts of money are involved in the news business. Although newspaper revenue has fallen, *USA Today* and *The Wall Street Journal* have increasing circulation. Cable news commands the majority of the money. Fox News Channel alone brought in nearly $800 million in revenue in 2013. Clearly, there's money to be made by giving us what we *want* instead of what we *need*.

However, a successful business model for a news organization does not necessarily lead to informed citizens or voters. When people complain about hyperbole and inaccuracies in news, they usually cite bias as their main concern. It's important to acknowledge that every news story comes from a specific point of view. If humans are writing and reporting the news, it's naïve to think it could be one hundred percent objective. I encourage my students to assume that *all* news sources are biased to some extent and to take everything with a grain of salt. But why do we assume that news should be objective? News media owe us nothing. They are not in public service; they exist to earn money for their stockholders.

"In the case of news, we should always wait for the sacrament of confirmation." —Voltaire

News consumers get themselves in real trouble when they engage in what media scholars call "selective exposure," meaning that viewers can choose news sources that affirm their already held beliefs. Since we don't like to be proven wrong—it causes cognitive dissonance and discomfort—it's easier to consume the Fox News product, if one is a conservative, or MSNBC's product, if one is a liberal. Facebook and Twitter are other popular vehicles for getting news. In fact, over thirty percent of American adults get their news from Facebook, amplifying the problems of selective exposure and inaccuracies.[6] If one only gets news from a single source, he is never exposed to other points of view. And as my students know—because I tend to jump up and down when talking about this in class—it's very important to get our news from multiple sources.

"We should at least be somewhat suspicious of the way that news sources, which otherwise expend considerable energy advertising their originality and independence of mind, seem so often to be in complete agreement on the momentous question of what happened today," writes Alain de Botton in his book *The News: A User's Manual.*[7] His insights raise an intriguing question, perhaps one that would make a good classroom media literacy project!

"News events are like Texas weather. If you don't like it, wait a minute." —Jessica Savitch

As I wrote earlier, we cannot change the news. We cannot change the senders of the news. But we *can* educate the receivers of the news to recognize the sources, tactics, and methods used to get and keep our attention.

Why Promote Media Literacy?

"Living in a 24-hour news cycle, with constant availability of media, media literacy is an important twenty-first century coping skill. Media literacy helps you filter the constant stream of information, helps you understand the messages you're receiving, and the motives of the content creators. If you're not being sold a product, you are the product, and media literacy helps you determine if you're the product."
–*Heather Melton, former student*

Media Literacy at Home:

- How do we, as a family, define news?

- Which sources of news do we consider the most credible?

- Are there stories we think should get more coverage but do not?

Media Literacy in the Classroom:

- How are news writing styles different than others? Hyperbole? Connotative words?

- Have news stories ever misrepresented groups of people or countries?

- In what ways can you fact check news stories?

- How does the format of the news change the story?

- What are ad prices in certain news outlets? Is it ethical for news to sell ad space?

QR CODES

Video: Standard News Reporting Formula (Language alert!)

New York Times News Photo Blog

PDF: Newspaper Critical Thinking Exercises

Walter Cronkite Announces Kennedy's Death – 38 Minutes Later

Center for News Literacy

News Literacy Project

Hilarious "The Onion" Spoof about TV News (Language alert!)

My Pinterest Board of News Mistakes

FOOTNOTES

1 Alain de Botton, *The News: A User's Manual* (New York: Pantheon Books, 2014), 137.

2 Eric Burns, *Infamous Scribblers: The Founding Fathers and the Rowdy Beginnings of American Journalism* (New York: PublicAffairs Publishing, 2007), 219.

3 Neil Postman, *Technopoly: The Surrender of Culture to Technology* (New York: Vintage Books, 1993), 70.

4 Alain de Botton, *The News: A User's Manual* (New York: Pantheon Books, 2014), 111.

5 Neil Postman, *Amusing Ourselves to Death: Public Discourse in the Age of Show Business* (New York: Penguin Books, 1985), 99.

6 Monica Anderson and Andrea Caumont, "How Social Media Is Reshaping News," *Pew Research Center*, September 14, 2014, http://www.pewresearch.org/fact-tank/2014/09/24/how-social-media-is-reshaping-news/.

7 Alain de Botton, *The News: A User's Manual* (n.p.: Hamish Hamilton, 2014), n.p.

6

BOOKS AND MAGAZINES

FACTS TO REMEMBER:

☛ Books are the oldest and most intimate mass medium.

☛ Books and magazines are the most narrowcasted, except for the Internet.

☛ Magazines print different editions for different areas and demographics.

Despite the popularity and prevalence of electronic media, we still place importance on printed material, like books and magazines. Strange. In contrast to other media sources, the printed word, particularly books and journals, holds instant, enduring, and sometimes unreasonable credibility. Before you buy in to what you read (even in this author's books), it makes sense to consider the source and impact of this intensely personal medium.

Once Upon a Time...

Printed material has been around since the days of papyrus and parchment, but it was the printing press—according to many media scholars—that changed the world.

Much has been written about the printing press's impact on society. From a media literacy perspective, the effects were significant because the printing press created the first *mass medium*. For the first time, the same message could be sent to many people at once. Pamphlets and books could be printed in large quantities. No longer did monks need to spend months copying an illuminated manuscript.

"Outside of a dog, a book is man's best friend. Inside of a dog, it's too dark to read." —Groucho Marx

Do you wonder if those first printing press operators realized the difference they made to the world? They were probably just excited about the machine's efficiency, but the impact of their work and this single technological advance cannot be understated. It made books and magazines more affordable and accessible, and, as a result, literacy rates increased.

The Magic of Books and Magazines

Every medium has a unique architecture that affects message delivery. This fact is particularly important to understand in regard to books and magazines.

Books

The book publishing industry is divided into three different branches: reference books, professional books, and trade books. Sales of reference books—dictionaries, maps, and encyclopedias—are dropping since this information is now on our smartphones. Professional books are leather-bound books you see on office shelves but are not commonly found in homes. Trade books are the ones we read and can be hardcovers, trade paperbacks, or mass-market paperbacks. Trade paperbacks are usually a bit bigger than the mass-market paperbacks, are printed on nicer paper, and are more durable. They also have the reputation of being a bit more highbrow than mass-market books. Interestingly, when J. K. Rowling finally got a contract for her *Harry Potter* books, she insisted the paperback versions only be printed in trade paperback.

Consuming a book is such a different experience from watching a television show or going to a movie. It's a personal and solitary event. It's intimate; we hold books close to us and use our imaginations to create mental images of the settings and characters. And although books are the oldest mass medium, they are still the most influential and diverse.

"A room without books is like a body without a soul." —Marcus Tullius Cicero

The magic of books lies in their intimacy and in the access they offer to an unlimited range of topics. Books have been written about every conceivable subject in the world. So just like cable channels, books *narrowcast*. No two book collections or personal libraries are exactly the same. This narrowcasting keeps the print industry afloat, even as our attention has turned toward electronic media.

Magazines

Walk into any library or bookstore and you will be greeted by an amazingly diverse selection of magazines covering specialized topics. You can find magazines for quilting, wooden boat building, cooking, diabetic cooking, low-carb cooking, gun collecting, model train building, and yoga. There is likely a magazine devoted to any hobby or interest imaginable; that variety helps keep magazines alive.

"You live several lives while reading." —William Styron

While the magazine experience is typically an individual one, we consume magazines more quickly than books and use less of our imagination doing so. Also, since the visual images encourage skimming, magazines are considered a "secondary medium" because we can read them while we watch television or listen to the radio.

Like books, the architecture of a magazine helps tell its story. Magazines can be identified by size (*Reader's Digest*) or by the trademark yellow frame on the cover (*National Geographic*). In fact, the shape and size of the magazine are just as important to its branding as any editorial content. *National Geographic* is printed on expensive and heavy high-quality paper so that the photographs are shown in the best possible way. The weight of *National Geographic*, for example, identifies the quality of the magazine as much as any article it contains. A magazine like *National Enquirer*, on the other hand, is printed on cheaper paper without a flat binding. One can almost predict the level of the content by the physical feeling of the magazine itself.

"Books are a uniquely portable magic." —Stephen King

The Business Side of Books and Magazines

Narrowcasting benefits the authors and readers, and it serves advertisers as well. In the late 1880s, magazines ceased to be content delivery systems and began focusing on delivering audiences to advertisers: specificity guaranteed ad sales. Instead of going for the largest possible audience, advertisers can find their niche market within the pages of magazines that target their ideal audience.

Magazine publishers take narrowcasting to an even finer point by printing different versions—called *split-run editions*—for different geographic areas or demographic groups. Magazines can then sell ad space to smaller, regional clients or aim ads at more lucrative demographic groups. The *TIME* magazine delivered in New York could be very different from the one delivered in Los Angeles. The *O, The Oprah Magazine* delivered to doctors could be different from the one delivered to schoolteachers. Like every other media source, the point of the magazine is to deliver ads to the right people, not necessarily to deliver content.

Several factors determine how much magazines charge for advertising space. Demographics (who reads the magazine) and circulation (how many subscribers it has and retail copies it sells) are important to advertisers. Because women make the bulk of purchasing decisions for the home and, thus, are a highly desirable audience for advertisers, ladies' magazines tend to be the most financially successful. That means *Better Homes & Gardens* or *Family Circle* can charge more for ad space than a magazine that might have a much higher circulation.

"Books are my friends, my companions. They make me laugh and cry and find meaning in life." —Christopher Paolini

Ad space prices *within* a magazine vary, depending on placement and size. The back cover is typically the most expensive advertising real estate in a magazine, followed closely by the inside front cover. As the page numbers of the magazine increase, the advertising prices decrease. You'll see huge spreads near the beginning of a magazine because those advertisers are willing to pay more for guaranteed visibility. The smaller and perhaps black-and-white ads near the back cost less, but they are also less noticeable to the reader.

Because they are so closely linked, it's nearly impossible to study magazines without studying their advertisers. Although it's easy to identify the target market of magazines based on their advertisers, it's also important to evaluate the editorial content to see how it relates to the advertised products. For example, if a fashion magazine didn't have articles telling us how we need to improve our appearance and style, would we feel as willing to try the products advertised within its pages? Before you buy that $1,500 dress or sign up for the diet plan that promises to give you the perfect body, think about how the articles you've read may have influenced designer lust or self-loathing. Fashion magazines, in particular, have much to gain by making readers feel inadequate and in constant need of improvement. The same principle applies to DIY, health and fitness, and hobby-specific magazines—they want to keep their advertisers happy. To do so, articles are often crafted to make you *want* specific products and brands.

Would you be surprised to know that the magazine with the highest circulation in the United States used to be *TV Guide*? It was the first magazine to recognize grocery stores as an excellent sales location. With show listings easily found on our televisions' channel guide or online, the magazine replaced the obsolete channel grid with features and pictures. Today, with its dwindling circulation (from 20 million at its peak to now hovering around 2 million), its management sees *TV Guide* as "a niche magazine for TV enthusiasts."[1] The magazines with the highest circulations today are actually free to the consumer and include AARP's *The Bulletin*, Costco's *Costco Connection* and Kraft's *Food & Family*. Sent out without any subscription fees, they make 100 percent of their revenue from advertising and function almost as public relations for the brand, rather than a magazine with actual editorial content.

"Most women's magazines simply try to mold women into bigger and better consumers." —Gloria Steinem

The book publishing industry may not sell advertising space to niche marketers, but, since magazine and book publishing companies are owned by the same multi-national conglomerates that own other media, their focus is still on the bottom line. Manuscripts sent to acquisition editors, the ones who determine which authors receive book contracts, are judged on their ability to sell.

A Permanent, Yet Evolving Industry

When radio and television started to overtake print media, there was concern the printed word would die out. Predicting the death of newspapers is somewhat of a sport for pundits, some of whom thought the last newspapers would be recycled as early as 2017.[2] But print media is tangible—we can hold it, fold it, carry it with us, smell it, and save it. In fact, many of my students say that, if they love a book on their electronic reading device, they will still buy a physical copy to keep. Books and magazines have a sense of permanency about them—especially in doctors' waiting rooms, where the magazines are usually years old!

"One thing I learned working at magazines was that, if you couldn't get people to look at a page or the cover, then you were fired."
—Barbara Kruger

Technology has made book publishing possible to those who hadn't considered it before. Self-publishing and e-publishing make producing books possible even without a traditional publisher. A few years ago, one of my students, Nathaniel, did just that. He was a small kid, probably 120 pounds dripping wet. He insisted that we call him "Danger," which I took to be strictly ironic and, although he didn't speak up much in class, he never missed a day.

After the class period when we talked about the history of the publishing industry, he asked if I'd be willing to read his manuscript—a diary of the time he served in Afghanistan. After hugging him and thanking him for his service (and coming to terms with the fact that this "kid" was actually not a kid at all), I told him I would be honored.

The manuscript—250 loose-leaf pages—arrived by FedEx the next day. While I realized I was committed to reading it, I wasn't in the mood at the time, but I started with page one. I turned the last page three hours later. Danger's story was moving, exciting, intriguing, and interesting. He was a fantastic storyteller, and he made his experiences in Afghanistan come to life. A few months later, I received another package from Danger: his book—a signed hardcover with his photo on the front. It was beautiful.

I tell my students this story because I never want them to think that writing books is something "other people" do. We can *all* do it. We all have stories to tell, and I don't want my students to feel limited because they believe they are too young, too inexperienced, or can't get published.

Writing books and articles allows everyday people and celebrities alike to share their stories and wisdom. Reading empowers to us with information and allows us to use our imaginations to create worlds in our heads. Words printed on a page aren't quite as direct as films or television; they leave the details to us. I appreciate Karen Marie Moning's take on the power the printed word gives us:

> I love books, by the way, way more than movies. Movies tell you what to think. A good book lets you choose a few thoughts for yourself. Movies show you the pink house. A good book tells you there's a pink house and lets you paint

some of the finishing touches, maybe choose the roof style, park your own car out front. My imagination has always topped anything a movie could come up with.[3]

We are apt to believe the words of nonfiction authors simply because we can hold their books in our hands. And with fiction, we feel like the characters are *ours*—our intimate friends. Do you know which class discussion usually upsets my students the most? The one about movie adaptations of their favorite books. They never feel the movies do the books justice. They feel insulted and disappointed.

"There's no mistaking a real book when one meets it. It's like falling in love." —Christopher Morley

We own our reading experiences more than any other. For this reason, books will be around forever. And because the experience of a book or magazine is often so personal, this medium deserves special analysis.

Why Promote Media Literacy?

"I think the engagement of critical thinking comes from asking students to constantly question the messages that we consume. What's the message? Who's conveying that message? And for what purpose? Media literate individuals start to ask the real questions, and I think that's where consumers start to become healthy skeptics." *–Tim Kohler, high school English teacher and former student*

Media Literacy at Home:

- In what way is reading a book different from consuming other media?

- How do movie versions of books change the story?

- Do you think books will always be around? Why or why not?

- We assume most magazine shots are doctored? Do our kids?

Media Literacy in the Classroom:

- How have books brought about social change?

- Have there been movie versions of books that your students didn't like? Why?

- Can you identify the target market of a magazine by its ads alone?

- Research magazine ad prices. How/why are they different?

QR CODES

**Website: Secrets of
Magazine Cover Design**

Magazine Design Site

Magazine Advertisement Gallery

FOOTNOTES

---

[1] Keith J. Kelly, "Changes in Store for TV Guide," *New York Post* (New York), June 26, 2014.

[2] Martin Bryant, "When Will Newspapers Die Out In Your Country?" *TNW News*, November 1, 2010, http://thenextweb.com/media/2010/11/01/when-will-newspapers-die-out-in-your-country-check-this-infographic/.

[3] Karen Marie Moning, *Darkfever* (New York: Delacorte Press, 2006), n.p.

7
ADVERTISING

FACTS TO REMEMBER:

- ☛ Advertising pays for the media we consume.
- ☛ Advertising caters to our emotions by attaching feelings to products.
- ☛ Advertising promotes an aspirational lifestyle.

Crass, loud, and ubiquitous, advertising is easy to criticize. It encourages materialism and overconsumption and entices us to buy products we don't need. (At least I didn't need that pink Venus razor until the commercial told me I couldn't live without it.) Advertising constantly reminds us that whiter teeth, shinier hair, or Uncle Ben's rice are the key to romance—which is why I tell my students that advertisers must think all consumers are superficial and silly.

In the previous chapter, we talked about how magazines evolved from content delivery devices to ad delivery devices. One can look at all media products, including television, radio, film, and Internet that way. Media is less about creating a product that will appeal to the market and more about creating a product that delivers the right market to advertisers. That said, much of the mass media we enjoy would not exist without the help of advertising dollars. Advertising makes magazines, radio stations, newspapers, and television channels possible and affordable. So, as much as we love to hate it, we need advertising.

"Advertising is the art of convincing someone to spend money they don't have on something they don't need." —Will Rogers

As irritating as marketing interruptions can be, I would argue that some of the most creative and talented people in the world work in advertising. Think of it this way: a film director has two hours to tell a story to a captive audience. A television writer has at least a few minutes to hook the viewer. An ad writer, however, must grab her target's attention within *seconds*. Not only is the ad writer working against the clock, but it takes something truly creative and clever to cut through the advertising clutter that inundates us daily.

It's fascinating that, although most people agree that advertising affects society, very few admit that advertising actually affects *them*. This *third-person effect* is quite a stumbling block to media literacy. Why should anyone study advertising, for example, if he doesn't think it affects him personally? Learning about advertising and how it works, though, is one of the most interesting aspects of becoming media literate.

A Targeted Approach

The first advertising agencies in the United States were nothing more than brokers who bought newspaper ad space in bulk at a discounted rate and then sold the space to businesses. It wasn't until brands became popular and marketers began to study demographics that agencies got involved in the creation of the ads. Demographics are the basic facts about consumers: gender, race, marital status, income, education level, zip code, religion, sexual orientation, etc. Demographics change throughout a person's life, and companies know this and have learned to adjust their advertising placement accordingly.

What's even more important to advertisers than demographics is a person's *psychographics*—his or her fears and desires. Psychographics help advertisers understand what make people tick. Once advertisers know their target market's demographics, they can surmise its psychographics and create ads that engage and influence a specific buyer.

Once advertisers determine the target market for an ad, psychographics come into play. Marketers ask questions such as:

- What's the best way to sell this product to this group?
- What is this group afraid of?
- What problem will this product solve for them?
- And, most importantly, what *feeling* can be attached to the use of this product?

The feelings associated with advertised products are called *appeals*, and the appeals make all the difference in how a product is viewed. Effective ads don't sell products; they sell *feelings*. For example, a razor—normally associated with daily drudgery—is presented as something *fun* to use. Need confidence? Make sure you apply the right deodorant. Afraid of not having enough money to retire? Choose the right money manager to help secure your financial future. Want to feel successful? Buy a certain type of car. Look no further than the perfume counter at a department store, and you'll be convinced that feelings play a role in branding and advertising. You'll see Clinique's *Happy*, Ralph Lauren's *Romance*, Estée Lauder's *Beautiful* and *Spellbound*, and Calvin Klein's *Euphoria* and *Endless Euphoria*. Who wouldn't want to experience these feelings? Great advertisers know how to appeal to our desires.

Fear, success, novelty, guilt, accomplishment, and, occasionally, humor, are the most common appeals used in advertising. And just like the media placement varies to reach specific demographics and psychographics, advertisers know they have to use different appeals to influence their potential buyers.

Most of my students who become advertising majors initially assume all ad campaigns for a particular product are identical. That is absolutely not the case. Depending on the target demographic group, ads for a single product are changed. For example, military recruiting ad aimed at parents might be very stark with basic information and appear in *TIME* or another general news magazine. An ad aimed at potential military recruits might emphasize adventure or danger and appear in *Rolling Stone*. While the product is the same, the techniques used in advertising it are not. Different types of ads work for different groups. The "bandwagon appeal"—everyone else has one—works much better with teenagers than it does for middle-agers who aren't as affected by peer pressure. The "plain folks pitch" might work for senior citizens, but it wouldn't work for middle schoolers. Celebrity spokespeople are much more effective with middle schoolers than with senior citizens, unless the celebrity was Andy Griffith, who could sell my parents anything!

"Many a small thing has been made large by the right kind of advertising." —Mark Twain

Using intense market analysis and research, advertisers constantly work to ensure their ads stay current with the desires and fears of their target markets. Once an ad campaign is developed, it's presented to a focus group. A focus group, made up of the same demographic as the target market, provides feedback to the ad agency. I encourage my students to participate in focus groups every chance they get. The process can be an excellent learning experience, and they'll get paid for their time and opinions!

Ad agencies use focus group results to tweak the campaign and may test it again before the media buyer takes over. The media buyer's job—which I think would be such fun—is to analyze media options and then spend other people's money to buy space in those outlets! When I show my students ads that they've never seen because they're targeted at demographic groups other than college students, I explain they have the media buyer to thank. Media buyers are the reason truck ads are placed in *Sports Illustrated* but not aired during *The Bachelor*, and why Mountain Dew advertises on MTV but not during *Jeopardy!*. Of course, narrowcasted cable channels have made media buying much easier!

Media buyers have thousands of choices on the Internet. Website cookies can tell marketers exactly what type of consumer you are and where you spend your time online. Media buyers pay more for ad space on "sticky" sites, meaning a web user is likely to stay on that site for a long time. They will also pay extra for sites with "clicks," which signify loads of web traffic. Since the Web is narrowcasted more than any other medium, advertisers can be extremely specific when buying time on sites. Not only is this good for advertisers, but it also increases the chance that a consumer will encounter an ad relevant to her.

Sex and Stereotypes in Advertising

While I have loads of criticisms about ads, I hate a cliché *about* advertising more than any ad itself. "Sex sells" unhinges me because people constantly repeat the phrase without really thinking about what it means. *Why* exactly does sex sell, and why is sex so often used to get our attention? The reason is because human beings are sexual by nature. Sex is the one thing that transcends every demographic and psychographic. And with consumers bombarded with ads—some say, on average, more than three thousand per day—isn't it wise for advertisers to cut through the clutter with something that everyone, regardless of age or income, will notice?

Nevertheless, sex in advertising can indeed have negative effects, leading to the objectification of women, the continuation of gender stereotypes, or the trivialization of relationships. Many ads feature women as objects: robots, mannequins, ice cream cones, or a pair of scissors. While it may sound ridiculous, once you notice, it's impossible to stop noticing. Media critic Jean Kilbourne claims this objectification of women's bodies—seeing them as things rather than as people—can lead to sexual abuse.[1] When I mention Kilbourne's work in class, I get some eye-rolls. Honestly, that was my initial reaction to her claims as well. However, when you consider that people see an enormous number of ads—every day, every year—perhaps Kilbourne's suggestion isn't unreasonable. After all, while seeing one ad objectifying women may not make a difference in someone's opinion of women, the cumulative, long-term effect of seeing millions of these types of ads could have a lasting and negative impact.[2]

"Advertising is fundamentally persuasion, and persuasion happens to not be science but an art." —William Bernbach

Gender stereotypes can appear in advertising in the form of dismemberment. For example, in most cases, men's bodies pictured in ads are shown as complete bodies. Women's bodies, however, are shown in pieces: lips, hair, feet, nails, legs, or teeth. What difference does this make? It suggests that the female form is irrelevant as a whole; it is merely the sum of its parts. While Kilbourne would claim this as another dimension of objectification, I see it more as a marketing ploy. Advertisers are smart to present women's bodies as pieces of a whole so that women always have some part that needs improvement. Do you think you have nice hair? Great! But your teeth need to be white as well! Do you have nice legs? Good, but better make sure your breasts are large enough and your skin is flawless! And once advertisers have focused our attention on our flaws, they offer us the perfect remedy. *Aren't we lucky?*

The most important thing media consumers can do is simply be aware of how female body image is portrayed in the media, specifically in advertising, and realize that the standard of beauty presented is unrealistic and unattainable. Advertising photos are almost always doctored for the best effect—even the models don't really look like their photos. Do a quick online search for before-and-after photographs of supposedly *perfect* models. You'll discover loads of photos that show these women (and men) aren't so perfect after all. Sharing these photos with others is a great way to start a conversation about the difference between *perfect* and *real.*

"Advertising is the greatest art form of the 20ᵗʰ century." —Marshall McLuhan

Stereotypes are also seen in how genders are represented when compared to each other. This is one of the most interesting aspects of ad analysis. I challenge you to find a fashion magazine that does *not* contain an ad featuring a solitary man, photographed in black and white, and looking extremely thoughtful or serious. Not an easy exercise. Then look for a full-color ad where women are featured in a group doing something silly. This is a very easy exercise. What difference does this make? It's cumulative effect again. What are thousands of these images teaching us about how genders behave? Men are independent and without emotion. And girls? Well, they just want to have fun. While it's easy to dismiss these as superficial examples, we must remember that we see over three thousand ads a day—most of them visual images. While flipping through a single fashion magazine likely won't impair gender perception, the sheer pervasiveness of these images deserves awareness and analysis.

Is It *Real?*

The "snob effect" is another popular advertising technique. Think of it this way: does a designer purse do anything that a plastic sandwich bag does not? No. Yet our brand-obsessed culture encourages us to spend hundreds of dollars for the purse, when a sandwich bag would hold all our personal items for a fraction of the cost. Branding is significant in advertising and in our culture in general. My students willingly admit they are irrationally devoted to particular brands and acknowledge they can't explain why. This is the power of branding and advertising.

Branding contributes to the idea that advertising creates an "aspirational lifestyle." Fashion magazines are often criticized for representing a lifestyle that is unattainable to most because of economic level or body type. Alexandra Shulman, editor of the British edition of *Vogue* since 1992, said in a BBC interview, "nobody wants to see a real person looking like a real person" in her magazine.[3] Magazines are brilliant at presenting a fantasy of perfection and wealth and then including ads for products or brands that make us feel like part of the fantasy. In his book *Present Shock*, Douglas Rushkoff analyzes this idea and writes of the aspirational lifestyle, "The consumer must never be allowed to reach his goal, for then his consumption would cease. Since consumption makes up about half of all economic activity in America, a happy consumer would spell disaster. Fashion must change, and products must be upgraded and updated."[4] If we can encourage students to realize this never-ending, unattainable pattern of more, bigger, and better, they will become critical consumers of the ads that surround them.

Brands are so pervasive in our society that many logos and even *colors* of logos are recognizable—even without the text or brand name attached. Scientists have determined that using certain colors in logos and brand packaging can actually influence consumers. Blue implies strength and dependability. Red means excitement! Yellow demonstrates optimism, clarity, and warmth. Green suggests peacefulness and health. Think about brand logos that you know. Do the colors used match the desired appeal of the brand?

Brand loyalty isn't necessarily a bad thing. We all have our favorite brands—mine's Diet Coke! But taking a step back to evaluate *why* we feel loyal to brands is one step toward media literacy.

Is It Love?

Intense brand loyalty leads to another criticism of advertising: It encourages us to have relationships with products rather than with people. We are told to love a Chevy or fall in love with a new product. A lipstick is described as "love at first swipe" (Revlon), and a gum flavor lasts so long it's our new "best friend" (Extra). A biscotti ad describes a cookie as "rugged, Italian, and easy to undress" (Nonni's Biscotti), while an overly excited woman holds a large version of the cookie. Another ad shows a woman eating Shredded Wheat next to her sleeping husband because "only the Shredded Wheat knows how to satisfy." Even a paint ad suggests you "fall in love with your walls" (Icynene) and features a photograph of a woman caressing her walls with her back arched. That must be some sexy paint! Once you start noticing these suggestive ads, you can't *stop* noticing. They are everywhere—and it's brilliant advertising. Ads like this play on our deepest emotional need—to love and be loved.

"Half the money I spend on advertising is wasted; the trouble is, I don't know which half." —John Wanamaker

Much is being written today about how digitally connected—yet lonely—we are, how personal relationships are being replaced with digital ones, and how this reality affects us mentally and emotionally. Advertisers play on our disconnected, dissatisfying relationships by suggesting, "Well then, how about a product on which you can always rely?" Ads promise that their product won't let you down like a silly human might. For example, a television ad for Kia Motors portrays a showroom as a dating website. Viewers are encouraged to log on, say what kind of relationship they want, and find their "love companion." The word "car" is never mentioned. My students typically make fun of this ad for being over the top, but then we step back to take another look. Don't we all have relationships with our cars? Some people even name them. In fact, as a joke one semester, I set up a Facebook page for my van, complete with profile name (Pearl Smith), hobbies (carpools), and an identifying statement ("Typically filled with empty Diet Coke cans and 80s music"). Once Pearl Smith's page reached a thousand views, I deleted it because it just seemed too ridiculous. However, the idea that we have relationships with products is valid.

We "love" our cars almost as much as our smartphones. An ad for an LG phone encourages the reader to "hold me, stroke me, touch me—you can't be without me." Seems outlandish, right? However, my students are *never* without their phones. Many sleep with their phones, and some can even text without taking their phones out of their pockets. Their phones are touching a part of their bodies at all times. So is it really unreasonable to say their primary relationship is with their phones? Smart advertisers know (and try to exploit the fact) that people love their phones.

> ## "The secret of all effective advertising is not the creation of new and tricky words and pictures, but one of putting familiar words and pictures into new relationships."
> ## —Leo Burnett

Advertisers encourage us to have relationships with products and, at the same time, urge us to trivialize real relationships. Look no further than the commercial for Carvel ice cream cakes, in which a dad tells his daughter to make a wish. As she blows out each birthday candle, the people at the table fall over and die one by one: Dad, Mom, Grandma, Little Brother. Satisfied, the young girl pulls the cake to herself while the tagline reads, "You won't want to share." JOOP! Jeans has an ad that claims, "A child is the ultimate pet." An ad for a jewelry company pictures a woman sitting with her legs closely held together—until a diamond ring is placed in front of her, and then her legs open. One ad for the JC Penney wedding registry says, "Marriage is about commitment. Marriage is about companionship. Marriage is about toaster ovens." These ads imply we are superficial and desperate for *things* instead of *people*—that we are lonely and only *stuff* can satisfy our loneliness. While it's an powerful marketing tactic, hopefully as you and your students begin to notice the fallacy of these ads, they will lose their efficacy.

The same personification tactic exists in branding as well. For example, many liquor brands have the names of *people*: Jose Cuervo, Jim Beam, Gentleman Jack, Johnnie Walker, Captain Morgan, and Jack Daniels. By presenting liquor to us as *friends*, companies communicate the message that we never have to drink alone. These *friends* are always available and ready to spend time with us.

Another way advertisers connect with buyers is by using the association principle. Companies associate their brands with things already valued in our culture, giving the brand instant credibility. The association principle is frequently used in ads for alcohol. For example, these ads usually feature gorgeous models having a wonderful time in fantastic, exotic locations. Additionally, one interesting campaign for Bacardi implied that the liquor would change your personality. You may be a banker by day, the ads claim, but you're "Bacardi by night." Bacardi's claim is sadly ironic, considering that liquor does indeed change people's personalities and not necessarily for the better.

No one uses the association principle better than the Budweiser brands of AB InBev, formerly Anheuser-Busch. During a past Super Bowl, they ran an ad featuring soldiers arriving in an airport. Other passengers slowly begin to clap for them, and close-ups of some of the soldiers show they are close to tears. This thirty-second ad spotlights American heroes and support of our military and ends with the Budweiser logo. The latent message—*Love our country, love Budweiser*—connects the brand with patriotism.

Targeting Minors

Alcohol companies are restricted from specifically advertising to minors. Nevertheless, the Federal Trade Commission (FTC) reported that, in 2014, nearly thirty percent of the alcohol industry's advertising dollars went to traditional media, like television, print, and radio—media that draw a high percentage of underage viewers. The FTC requires that at least 71.6 percent of the traditional media audience of an alcohol advertisement be over twenty-one years old, but how is that condition monitored or quantified? Likewise, expenditures for online alcohol ads have tripled.[5] To comply with restrictions about advertising to underage viewers, the websites containing these ads are "age gated," meaning one must enter her age before she can access the entire site. However, does your keyboard know how old *you* are? The "age gate" defense seems risky at best.

"It is advertising and the logic of consumerism that governs the depiction of reality in the mass media." —Christopher Lasch

In a more recent Super Bowl ad, Budweiser once again used the association principle. What does everyone love? *Puppies*—and the Budweiser Clydesdales! Their latest ads involve a story with *both*. When I show this commercial during alcohol/tobacco advertising workshops for high school students, as soon as the puppy comes on, half of the students say, *"Awwwwww,"* taking the bait—hook, line, and sinker! They watch a cute story about a puppy without realizing they're actually watching an advertisement for a product that accounted for nearly one-third of traffic related deaths in 2012.[6]

Tobacco advertisers are also prevented by law from targeting teens. But, since more than 1,300 smokers die daily,[7] the tobacco industry desperately needs replacement smokers. Their challenge, however, is that someone who reaches the age of eighteen without smoking is unlikely to ever smoke. Consequently, teens comprise the future market for tobacco companies.

To get around the law, tobacco companies place huge displays at convenience stores, implement direct mail campaigns, sponsor sporting events, and advertise in youth-oriented magazines. R. J. Reynolds actually put ads in the classroom editions of *TIME* magazine in 2003! Tobacco companies also have a large online presence, which they claim is acceptable because they also use age gates. Additionally, they use merchandise giveaways, including lip gloss and cell phone case stickers, which don't seem like giveaways that would appeal to women over eighteen.

Studying magazine ads for cigarettes is almost like participating in a sociology course in which issues such as class struggle, government intervention, and even conflicts between the genders come to light. For instance, the Centers for Disease Control reports that a person is more likely to be a smoker if he or she is uneducated and poor. Advertisers know this and present cigarettes as something to soothe job stress. For example, an ad for Capri cigarettes shows a woman relaxing with a cigarette and states, "She's gone to Capri, and she's not coming back." Or tobacco is shown as a power tool: a maid, who clearly dislikes her job, appears ready to flick the ashes of her Camel cigarette into her boss's food. A few years ago, the Virginia Slims campaign encouraged women to "find your voice," implying that cigarettes made that possible. That's ironic, since throat cancer robs people of their voices.

Cigarettes are also shown as tools of independence. Winston's ad challenged smoking restrictions by stating, "At least you can still smoke in your car." The Virginia Slims slogan, "You've come a long way, baby," celebrates women's choices and independence. Ironically, the ads mention nothing about how the smoker becomes addicted to nicotine. And nothing says independence like the classic Marlboro Man—the quintessential American cowboy—rugged, cocky, and masculine. Sadly, four of the original Marlboro men died from smoking-related illnesses.

Ever notice how some cigarette brands are called *slims* or *super slims*? That's not accidental. For years tobacco has been pitched to users as an appetite suppressant. Hungry? Have a "slim" instead of a snack. Typically *slim* cigarettes are even manufactured to be skinnier and longer than a normal cigarette.

Media literacy expert Art Silverblatt states that tobacco advertisers are the most talented in the industry. "How else could they encourage us to do something that no one actually enjoys the first time they try it?" he frequently asks.

Class discussions about tobacco and liquor advertisements are usually pretty lively. One or two students usually insist that all of these ads should be illegal because "the product is bad for us." Another student will invariably say, "Then McDonald's ads should be outlawed too." It's a slippery slope with some significant First Amendment considerations. After all, smoking and drinking *are* legal activities as long as you're a certain age.

Media literacy can play a huge role in these issues. We can teach teens to be smarter than the ads and teach them the tricks and techniques the advertisers are using to make these activities more exciting and glamorous than they really are. We can also help them evaluate the appeals being used by the companies. Some say peer pressure—not tobacco advertising—plays the major role in a teen's decision to begin smoking. Perhaps so, but advertising must be somewhat effective for the industry to spend over $8.2 billion on it annually.

Advertising is a huge part of our culture, and most of our media would not exist without it. Because it is so pervasive, powerful, and emotive, we need to analyze it. Awareness is the first step, followed by criticism and evaluation. Media literacy can even increase our appreciation of fantastic ad campaigns. But awareness must come first. While we can't outlaw advertising and we can't avoid it, we can *outsmart* it.

Why Promote Media Literacy?

"I strongly believe that media literacy is important because it protects you from any negative influences of the media. Media literacy has built my communication skills tremendously and my interpretation of media messages. Being media literate allows me to view the world in such a realistic and practical way. Because of media literacy, I can no longer read magazines or view commercials the same way, and I no longer automatically believe everything that pops up over social media or TV." *–Krystal Wilson, former student*

Media Literacy at Home:

- Which ads are effective with our family? Why?

- Do we notice the word and model choices of ads, and their intent?

- Are there ads that make us feel like we are inadequate or missing out? Is that true?

Media Literacy in the Classroom:

- What types of pervasive words or techniques are used in advertising?

- How do advertisers use psychology?

- How much does an ad typically cost?

- What can ads from the past teach us about cultural changes?

QR CODES

Website: Brand Logo Alphabet Game

How Is the Music Different in Ads for Girls Versus Ads for Boys?

Video Clip: TV Product Placement Examples

Pinterest Page of Photoshop Clips and Funny Spoofs

Video Clip: Behind the Scenes of a McDonald's Commercial

Duke University Ad Library

Google Doc: List of TV Commercials Worth Watching and Analyzing

FOOTNOTES

[1] Jean Kilbourne, *Deadly Persuasion: Why Women and Girls Must Fight the Addictive Power of Advertising* (New York: Free Press, 1999). Also published as Jean Kilbourne, *Can't Buy My Love: How Advertising Changes the Way We Think and Feel* (New York: Free Press, 2000).

[2] "Advertising and Sexual Assault: The Relationship Between Advertising, Gender Roles, and Sexual Assault," last modified April 1, 2010, http://blog.lib.umn.edu/brun0305/advertisingandsexualassaulttherelationshipbetweenadvertising,gender-roles,andsexualassault/2010/04/advertising-gender-roles-and-sexual-assault-1.html.

[3] Jenn Selby, "'No-one Wants to See a Real Person on the Cover of Vogue,' Says British Vogue Editor Alexandra Shulman," *The Independent* (London), March 17, 2014.

[4] Douglas Rushkoff, *Present Shock: When Everything Happens Now* (New York: Current, 2013), n.p.

[5] Federal Trade Commission, "Self-Regulation in the Alcohol Industry" (Appendix B: Alcohol Advertising Expenditures, 2014), iii.

[6] "Traffic Safety Facts," (U.S. Department of Transportation, 2013), 1-2.

[7] "Fast Facts," Centers for Disease Control, accessed June 13, 2015, http://www.cdc.gov/tobacco/data_statistics/fact_sheets/fast_facts/index.htm#toll.

8
THE INTERNET

FACTS TO REMEMBER:

- ☞ If you are using a free website, then you are the product being sold.
- ☞ It's critical to evaluate information for truth and authenticity.
- ☞ Sites use your information to place particular ads on other sites you visit.
- ☞ Social media can affect your self-perception.

I still remember the first time I accessed an Internet message board. I was a graduate student using one of the school's computers. After the prolonged series of clicks, beeps, and static bumps of the dial-up modem, I logged onto the message board. With its plain formatting and pixilated Courier font, it wasn't fancy, but I was impressed. Seeing posts on the board from people in Iceland blew my mind! There I was in Illinois, and I could write a note to someone on the other side of the globe—words that, if anyone was awake to see them, could be read instantly. My students laugh when I imitate the sound the dial-up modem made (You remember it, too!), mostly because they have grown up with the Internet in their pockets. They can't imagine anything less than instant access to any kind of information imaginable. The Internet doesn't excite them; it's simply a fact of their everyday lives.

"The Internet is becoming the town square of the global village of tomorrow." —Bill Gates

The Internet is different from all forms of media because all other forms converge online. We can watch movies, read papers and books, catch up on news, or binge on television shows all through an online connection. It's also where we—the users—have the most input. While this diversity of content and voices gives the Internet its amazing vitality, it also makes media literacy all the more important. How do we begin to analyze the terabytes of information—much of it user-generated and not all of it accurate—from thousands of sources? We can start by understanding how the Internet began.

The Birth of the Internet

Four months after the Soviets launched the Sputnik satellite in 1957, President Eisenhower created the Advanced Research Projects Agency (ARPA) to help the United States catch up in the space race.

ARPA consisted of engineers and computer scientists who created the first network of computers which they called ARPANET. ARPANET comprised only *four* computers. Later, other computers around the country, especially at research universities and corporations, tapped into the network. By the 1970s, the computers were communicating by radio waves instead of phone lines. This communication was called "inter-networking"—*Internet* for short.

The World Wide Web wasn't born until 1990, when Tim Berners-Lee developed a navigating system for this network. Most people mistakenly think the Internet and the Web are the same thing, but the Web is actually the vehicle used to travel around the Internet. The Internet is the structure—the hardware, servers, wires, and waves that contain and carry information from one computer to the next. The Web is the way the information is organized and accessed.

Advertising Directly and Specifically to You

The Internet narrowcasts more than any other medium, which enables *anyone* to find a home online—even if his or her hobbies and tastes are obscure. And through cookies and special-interest websites, advertisers can target and reach any consumer. Although you don't pay for access to most of the websites you use, this home isn't free. The fact to remember is that, if you aren't paying to use a website, then *you* are the product being sold. As with any other media today, the Internet exists to deliver people to advertisers, not to deliver content to people. Every search you do or website you visit gives the Internet information about yourself, which enables companies to target you like never before. The ads that appear on your Facebook page, for example, are directly related to *you*. Did you post something about wanting to travel? Hotel ads will show up in your feed. Did you change your relationship status to *single*? Ads for weight-loss products and anti-depressants may appear on your wall. This technology could potentially mean you never see an ad for a product that does not interest you. It's brilliant marketing! But from a media literacy standpoint, you, as the consumer, really need to pay attention.

Changing the Way We Access and Share Information

The convergence of media online has created some challenges for traditional mass media formats. My students, for example, watch television content online through streaming services. Why should they sit in front of a TV at a certain time when they can click a mouse and watch what they want, whenever they want? Movie distributors face a similar challenge. Since movies tend to be released digitally so soon after they appear in theaters, some people skip the overpriced popcorn and just wait to stream the films at home. And no medium has suffered at the hands of the Internet more than print. Although electronic books are still sold and read through a myriad of devices, newspaper circulation has dropped drastically. Much like record labels that missed the chance to maximize on digital music sales when Apple created iTunes, the newspaper industry shot itself in the foot when papers began to distribute content freely online. Why would people *pay* for news that's ten hours old when it's immediately available online from the same source for *free*?

Online experiences differ from other media in a variety of ways. We can communicate with other people—it's interactive, it's global, and its content is portable and sometimes user-generated. But the most interesting aspect of the Internet is the ability it gives us to call up content on demand. Technology makes on-demand access possible with television and music (think streaming services, DVRs, etc.), but your content choices, though varied, are still limited. On the Internet, *you* choose the content by choosing which sites to visit.

Any description of the connecting power of people and information on the Internet sounds like hyperbole—except it isn't an exaggeration to say I have friends *all over the world* because of online experiences and a shared passion for media literacy. How would that have been possible without the Internet? We may have had pen pals when we were younger, but the Internet provides an immediate and richer multi-media interaction.

Greater Potential, Greater Responsibility

We can take ownership of the Internet in a way that isn't possible with movies, magazines, or television programs. We have personal websites and our own social networking profiles—even our own YouTube channels. We are creating the Internet as much as we are consuming and sharing it. The Internet is essentially a huge laboratory of creativity shared by everyone who has a connection. But with this power to create comes enormous responsibility. No ombudsman stands guard over the Internet to tell us when something is inaccurate or unethical. The *good*, the *bad*, the *ugly*—it's all there on the Internet. Deciphering this glut of information for relevance and accuracy requires both critical thinking and hard work.

The culture of the Internet definitely demands that we be good *digital citizens*. What does that mean, exactly? Of the numerous definitions, my students' favorite is, "Don't be a jerk." Sounds good in theory, right? In practice, digital citizenship is not so easily implemented. The term "digital citizenship" first appeared on my radar in 2006, when a thirteen-year-old girl named Megan Meier committed suicide in a town not far from where I live. The mother of a former friend of Megan's had set up a fake MySpace profile as a boy named "Josh Evans" to spy on Megan. "Josh" and Megan chatted until she received a message from him saying the world would be better off without her. The comment elicited similar hurtful messages from other MySpace "friends" aimed at Megan. Not long after, Megan's mother found her hanged in her closet. Megan's suicide evolved into a huge news story about the impact of relationships in this new, online world. What was real? What was fake? And how was a thirteen-year-old girl to know the difference?

"If television is a babysitter, then the Internet is a drunk librarian who won't shut up." —Dorothy Gambrell

The question about what is real or fake resonates today. We have the freedom to create or say whatever we want online. Naturally, some people abuse that freedom and act in less than ethical ways. Since the news media tends to dramatize and accentuate stories to keep us watching, reports about the Internet often feature Megan Meier-type stories and warnings about identity theft and online predators. Rarely does a news story cover anything positive about the Internet in general or social media in particular.

Getting students to think critically about the Internet is challenging. It has been a part of their entire lives, and, while they know some of it is fake, they're uninterested. Want to see a group of students roll their eyes? Talk to them about *cyberbullying*. They've heard it all before and seen content in this Wild West environment, where no one is in charge. Personally, I think students are savvier consumers than we give them credit for being. Still, many aspects of the online experience require caution and reflection. For example, because students can take ownership of the Internet and build online identities, it's important for them to recognize how they present themselves. Educators can initiate the conversation by asking students how they *edit* themselves to present a specific image online. Do they build their profiles based on the site and its users? Are there any sites on which they are one hundred percent honest? Getting students to talk about how they craft their online personas may help them understand that the people they meet online may be just as carefully fashioned.

The Internet can be a place where we express ourselves in a variety of ways, but some might say that all of the focus on *self*, *identity*, and *selfie* leads to narcissism. In some cases, that may be true. What I worry about most, however, is the desperate need in some online communities for *affirmation*—in many cases, from strangers. Instagram, for example, allows users to post photos that their followers can either *like*, *comment* on, or, the worst, *ignore*. A running total of likes received shows up on the screen alongside the comments. Additionally, the number of followers a person has, as well as who those followers are, is public unless he has set his account to require people to have permission to see the posts. This is significant because it makes the social hierarchy quantitative and public. When we were in school, we knew a social hierarchy existed. But now with Instagram and other online sites, popularity has a number. Ask any middle-school girl how many Instagram or Twitter followers she has, and she can tell you the exact number at any time. Ask her the names of the *popular* girls she follows but who don't follow her back, and she'll know.

Instagram has become much more than just sharing photos; it's a tool teens today use to measure their worth and value. What's especially dangerous about this gauge is that posts do not represent how creative, intelligent, or generous they are. Instagram photos only represent their physical selves.

Twitter follows a similar structure to Instagram, but it's not primarily photos; students can post links, videos, or simple comments. Unlike Instagram, however, Twitter has no age requirement and no ban on nudity. A Twitter account can expose a student to many things for which they may not be prepared. Heck, Twitter sometimes exposes *me* to things I'm not prepared to see!

Snapchat is another way to connect with people, but its original marketing plan revolved around the fact that photos *disappear* after a certain number of seconds set by the sender. The receiver, however, can take a screenshot of the "snap" and then the sender is notified that a screenshot has been taken. What many students do *not* know, however, is that dozens of apps are available for permanently keeping snaps without the sender being aware. Snapchat's original reputation was for *sexting* racy photos. Thankfully, it seems to have evolved into something less risqué (and risky); many of my students use Snapchat simply for texting.

Other sites, including Tumblr, Vine, YouNow, and Reddit all involve posting and tallying responses. Social media will always offer new apps and sites that claim to be the *next big thing*, but my research and experience lead me to believe that Instagram, Twitter, and Snapchat are here for the long haul. Facebook, according to my students, is now only for "old" people. Apparently, we have taken it over and killed it for the young and hip!

"It is the greatest truth of our age; information is not knowledge." —Caleb Carr

The constant desire for affirmation from strangers is problematic, especially for Millennials and Generation Z, who have never experienced a world without social media and its constant count of likes and comments. When movements, like the one that involves posting videos of one's self on YouTube and tagging them with "Am I pretty or ugly?," determine how teens and young adults see themselves, society has a problem. The pull of the online experience can be so strong that people willingly invite negativity into their lives.

A Picture Is Worth 1,000 (Potentially Inaccurate) Words

Through any of these sites, photos fly around the Internet quickly, effortlessly, and pervasively. Once a photo is sent, it can never again be controlled—a lesson some only learn after a negative experience. Photos can be misappropriated and used by others without your knowledge or permission. My friend Bob is an extremely talented photographer who moonlights as a Batman cosplayer. He made a Robin costume for his son to wear at conventions. They also do a ton of charity work visiting kids in hospitals, etc. Not long ago, he sent me this photo, knowing that I'd be interested in its origins.[1]

Someone had seen it shared on *The Mommy Guide* Facebook page. Viewers were encouraged to "share this photo if you would do anything for your kids."[2]

Why did Bob want me to see this? Because while the photo itself is real, the story is a lie. Someone from *The Mommy Guide* found the image online and appropriated it for her own use. There was Bob— being used to promote a site he had never heard of. Interestingly, he wasn't upset. He simply thought it was slightly funny, since his son would have never worn the Robin costume to school for fear something would happen to it.

"You are what you share."
—C.W. Leadbeater

Two days after I received Bob's note, one of my students showed me an Instagram photo of her that had been used to advertise a "lesbian sex party." The photo had been downloaded from Instagram and placed in a Craigslist ad promoting the party at a particular address. It turned out that the post was a practical joke played on those who lived at the address. But the photo, stolen from the Web by strangers, was definitely of my student. She has since made her Instagram account private so that only people who have her permission can access her photos.

Getting Social

When we were younger, my friends and I used every method possible to keep up with one another; we talked in person, passed notes during class, and called each other on the phone. (Yes, the phones were attached to the kitchen wall by cords and you had to talk to your friends while your entire family was standing around you, but it's what we had!) Students today do the exact same thing to keep up with their friends; they just have a much larger set of tools available to them. Because the younger generation has integrated social media platforms and texting into their lives, many adults are concerned that students don't have a sense of what it actually means to be *social*. That might be true in some cases, but problems really only occur when they let their behind-the-screen networking skills overshadow their personal social skills.

"The Internet is just a world passing notes around a classroom." —Jon Stewart

On the first day of class, I do an experiment with my students. I ask them to introduce themselves to me and shake my hand as they leave the room. What I don't tell them is that I count how many of them give me a decent handshake with eye-contact. Over the past few years, an average of about forty percent do so. We spend a great deal of time during the semester, discussing social media use and its potential effects. On the last day of class, we shake hands again. I'm happy to report that the percentage of students who exhibit real-life social skills always increases! Simple awareness brings about change.

Students are not the only ones who over-rely on social media or use it inappropriately. We have all cringed at our friends' Facebook posts. Alongside the potential for misuse, social media offers benefits as well. These sites allow us to present ourselves in whatever way we choose, which, in some instances, is a positive thing. Nev Schulman, producer of MTV's program *Catfish*, points out, "They get attention and respect online that sometimes they don't get in real life."[3] Interestingly, *Catfish* is a documentary telling the story of his own ill-fated online relationship.

Scary stories about social media and various online experiences abound. I am frequently asked to speak to parent groups about ways to decrease cyberbullying. It's interesting to me that parents know about cyberbullying but can't name the apps their children have on their phones, much less explain what those apps do. Parents are hungry for solutions to protect their children, but they have no idea where to start. And sensationalized news media only exacerbate the issue. The problem with trying to fix online bullying is that we can't stop people from acting inappropriately. Perhaps I am a cynic, but I don't think parent-teacher meetings can keep kids (or their parents) from acting like jerks. Since we all have to deal with difficult people in *real life* situations, wouldn't it be a better use of time and resources to teach skills for coping with difficult people in our *online* experiences as well? We need to remember that social media and apps are tools; our experiences depend on how the tools are *used*. Because there will always be people who use these tools inappropriately, it's our job to make sure our kids and students are aware of what they are putting out into the world and prepared to respond *appropriately* to others' bad behavior.

Another potential challenge that is as problematic as bullying is how the Internet's immediacy affects our patience and attention spans. We *surf, click, glance*—we rarely have to wait for any bit of information we desire. Even songs, movies, and television programs are available within seconds. Is it possible for us to sit still... ever? Are we in constant need of entertainment and stimulation? Nicholas Carr writes in his book *The Shallows: What the Internet Is Doing to Our Brains*, "[T]he more we use the Web, the more we train our brain to be distracted—to process information very quickly and very efficiently but without sustained attention."[4] As we've previously discussed, we *know* a lot of facts, but we rarely know the *context* behind the facts. Carr claims that the Internet works as an external hard drive for our brains—anything we need to know or remember can be stored in the cloud, so why bother focusing?

"The Unending Anxiety of an ICYMI World," an article featured in *The New York Times*, addressed the feeling of constant panic caused by not being caught up on the barrage of social media. It's called *ICYMI* ("in case you missed it") *anxiety*, which can also lead to a severe case of *FOMO* ("fear of missing out").[5] We all had FOMO when we were growing up, but it was not a constant state. The pervasive nature of social media in the lives of our kids and students means they could potentially be dealing with FOMO at all times. Pressure indeed!

When I do workshops for middle schoolers about social media use and digital citizenship, I try to get them to reflect and analyze why they use the media and how it makes them feel. Here are some of the responses:

> *"Without Instagram, I would have no life."* —sixth grader
>
> *"I used to feel like I belonged; now without Instagram I feel left out."* —seventh grader
>
> *"Social media help me with my comunation."*
> —sixth grader
>
> *"All these apps are my life."* —eighth grader
>
> *"Social media cheer me up when I'm sad. So do cat videos."*
> —seventh grader

Workshops for high schoolers can be more problematic. Last year, I gave a talk about "digital footprints" at a suburban high school in St. Louis. Thinking I'd provide the students with an *aha* moment, I researched a few of them online, found some incriminating Instagram and Twitter photos of them, covered their faces, and included them in my presentation. I showed the slides to the students, hoping to illustrate how easy it was for me to find examples of irresponsible online behavior. Instead, the students cheered. One student, who was pictured holding a bottle of Jägermeister, stood up and hollered, "That's *me!*" while his classmates cheered. My plan backfired miserably, and I was left with two thoughts:

1. A level of maturity is required to actually care about one's digital footprint.

2. Perhaps "famous" and "infamous" are identical—and both desirable—to this generation.

Social media workshops for parents are also usually an adventure. If a parent's only knowledge of social media comes from local news stories, they will have misconceptions. Parents don't usually know that Twitter and Instagram accounts can be protected so that a student can only be followed by those who have permission. Most parents think that online predators are the biggest issue with social media. My attempts to convince them that a decreased attention span and an unreasonable desire for affirmation from strangers are *bigger* threats to their children's well-being typically fall on deaf ears. At least one parent in every workshop will demand that the "schools do something." Schools *are* implementing digital citizenship strategies across the country, but that effort is not enough. Students need to hear positive guidance from every source possible. Like Peter Parker was told, "With great power comes great responsibility." Giving a child a smartphone without conversations about responsibility and potential threats is as ridiculous as giving a teenager a Ferrari without first requiring him to take driver's ed.

"Only on the Internet can a person be lonely and popular at the same time."
—Allison Burnett

The Internet is magnificent! But like former Google CEO Eric Schmidt writes, "The Internet is the first thing that humanity has built that humanity doesn't understand, the largest experiment in anarchy we've ever had."[6] No one is supervising this enormous digital playground, so the importance of media literacy, when it comes to the Internet, cannot be overstated.

The Internet can be seen as a mirror reflecting who we are, or, perhaps, the image we would like to portray. We can build profiles of ourselves and others, we can search out any information we'd like, and ignore information that might be uncomfortable. We can be in touch and entertained at any minute of the day. Our kids and students have grown up in this world, and they deserve the chance to step back, reflect, and analyze how it has possibly affected them.

Why Promote Media Literacy

"The media is becoming an overwhelming presence in the day-to-day life of everyone, especially children and teens. Without media literacy, we will be raising a generation to believe the first article that shows up on their feed, rather than looking for any truth in anything. We will have millions of people walking around without the notion to think for themselves and believing everything the media wants them to believe." –*Candace Fee, former student*

Media Literacy at Home:

- Do we let social media affect how we perceive ourselves?

- In what ways are people different in real life?

- How can we determine which sites and people are real and trustworthy?

Media Literacy in the Classroom:

- How can we evaluate websites and sources for authenticity?

- What does it mean to be a good digital citizen?

- Imagine how historical figures may have used social media.

QR CODES

**Infographic:
History of Social Media**

**Infographic: A Teacher's Guide to
Social Media**

**TED Talk: How Social Media Have
Changed Relationships**

**Website: Nine Elements of
Digital Citizenship**

**PEW Report: Teens, Tech, and
Social Media**

FOOTNOTES

[1] Photo used with permission from Bob Kieffer.

[2] "The Mommy Guide," *Facebook*, accessed June 13, 2015, https://www.facebook.com/MommyGuide.

[3] Nev Schulman, conversation with the author, November 2013.

[4] Nicholas Carr, *The Shallows: What The Internet Is Doing to Our Brains* (New York, W. W. Norton & Company, Inc., 2010), 194.

[5] Teddy Wayne, "The Unending Anxiety of an ICYMI World," *The New York Times* (New York), January 2, 2015.

[6] Eric Schmidt and Jared Cohen, *The New Digital Age: Transforming Nations, Businesses and Our Lives*, (n.p.: Vintage Press 2014), i.

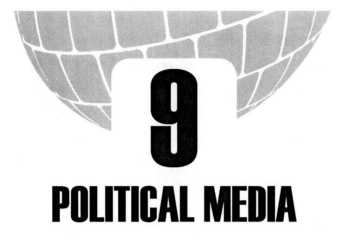

POLITICAL MEDIA

FACTS TO REMEMBER:

- ☞ Political coverage is primarily visual.
- ☞ A focus on image and drama takes the attention off policy issues.
- ☞ Anything goes with political commercials.
- ☞ Lack of media literacy can threaten democracy.

Who will you vote for in the next election? Chances are you don't know the candidates personally, so how will you learn about them? Will you watch debates on television? Read the newspaper editorials? Listen to talk shows on the radio? Follow the polls online? And how will you separate the truth from the mud that gets slung across all those media platforms?

Media literacy is a great skill to have when consuming television, movies, music, and advertising, but it is crucial when political communication is involved. Analysis of political coverage factors in everything we've discussed so far—the use of visuals, context (or lack thereof), money sources, and an awareness of how sensationalism is used. Media *illiteracy* in the political arena can actually threaten our democracy.

Popping Our Political Bubbles

Political information saturates the media, making it difficult for people to distinguish what is meaningful and true. In addition, as Michael Delli Carpini and Scott Keeter point out in their book, *What Americans Know about Politics and Why It Matters*, many voters are woefully ignorant about politics. The general public's inadequate knowledge of the political process, combined with a glut of information, challenges their ability to discern fact from falsehood.[1] People need media literacy!

In regard to politics, there is good news and bad news when it comes to media. The good news is that countless sources provide political news. The bad news is that countless sources provide political news. The availability of such varied and on-demand news choices also means that, instead of ideas and information being *pushed* on us at given times by trusted and well-established television anchors like Walter Cronkite, we can selectively *pull* news anytime we want from thousands of possible sources. Conservatives will most likely select news from conservative news outlets, and liberals from liberal news outlets. The irony is that, because we have so many options, we tend to limit what learn and never have to hear viewpoints that oppose our own.

Critics refer to this self-selection of information as the *political echo chamber*, insinuating that we validate our opinions by the news choices we select. This practice locks us into ideological bubbles; it also prevents us from finding any commonalities with those who disagree with us. As a result, political discourse in America has deteriorated from saying, "I'm right, you're wrong" to "I'm right, you're stupid."

I blame the decline of civil political discourse on the twenty-four-hour news cycle. News producers must fill each hour with visuals and stories to keep viewers engaged and interested. Very often, the programs tell us what we *want* to hear rather than what we *need* to hear. Therein lies the problem. We need the media to cover political news because very few of us actually get to meet or know our elected officials personally. We depend on the media to tell us about them. We forget that the media are profit-based institutions and are not responsible for public service. They are responsible for keeping our attention.

"Modern politics today requires a mastery of television." —Walter Mondale

Some accuse the media of shortening our attention spans. Given the constant stream of images and action that keeps our eyes, if not our thoughts, focused, that accusation is certainly understandable. On average, television programming runs for seven minutes before breaking for commercial. Compare those seven short minutes to the length of the first of the famous Lincoln/Douglas debates which took place on August 21, 1858. Douglas spoke for an hour, Lincoln replied for an hour and a half, and Douglas gave a half-hour rebuttal. A three-hour debate! What American voter today could handle that? Douglas even notes the intelligence and concentration of his audience by saying, "Silence will be more acceptable to me in the discussion of these questions than applause. I desire to address myself to your judgment, your understanding…and not to your passions or enthusiasms."[2]

Media literacy doesn't guarantee a longer attention span, but it can lead to awareness of how political messages are created and why. In turn, awareness can lead to critical consumption and even some political *curiosity*. Perhaps, most significantly, it can produce voters who are not swayed by passion or enthusiasm but by facts.

The Power of Visual Presence

My students struggle to imagine what it would be like to vote for public officials without first hearing or seeing them. In the past, politicians and statesmen were recognized by their *writings*. It must have been a treat for people to listen to Franklin Roosevelt's speeches on the radio and hear his voice in their own living rooms! What genius to name his broadcasts *fireside chats*, making them intimate and personal—like a friend sitting with you by the fire. Even when radio made it possible to speak directly to the public, Roosevelt gave only thirty-three fireside chats in eleven years. He understood even then that an overload of presidential messages lessens their significance.

Today, our culture is visual. While we'd still recognize the president's voice if we heard it on the radio, being telegenic is the most important trait a politician can have. Politicians and public figures *must* come across well on TV. The power of visual presence became obvious in the first televised presidential debate held between Richard Nixon and John Kennedy on September 26, 1960. Radio listeners thought Nixon won the debate; however, those who watched it on television believed Kennedy won. Did the medium make the difference? Kennedy was young, handsome, and tan. Nixon was recovering from the flu and still had a low fever. Kennedy looked into the camera when he answered questions; Nixon answered to the reporters in the room, which made him look shifty-eyed. Whether or not the debate made a difference in the election was hard to tell, but there was no question afterwards about the importance of a politician's presence on television.

"The velocity and knee-jerk response to events happening in real time that television brings us precludes any kind of reflection or contemplation." —Bill Viola

How many people today don't win—or even run for—public office because they are *not* telegenic? Consider Thomas Jefferson who was voted "homeliest scholar" at the College of William and Mary and who, because of a speech impediment, avoided speaking directly to Congress. Would he be elected today? Or what about William Howard Taft, who sweated profusely and weighed 305 pounds? Even Abraham Lincoln, whose voice rose an octave when he was nervous, was not immune.[3] Could Franklin Roosevelt have successfully campaigned and stood up against our World War II enemies from his wheelchair? Would any of these historic leaders have been elected in our telegenic culture? The importance of a candidate's visual image cannot be overstated. Writing about this without sounding critical is difficult, but I wonder how many potential leaders we've missed because they lacked visual appeal.

Steven Johnson, in his book *Everything Bad is Good For You*, defends television as a reliable gauge of political acumen, saying "When we see our politicians in the global living room of televised intimacy, we're able to detect more profound qualities in them: not just their grooming, but their emotional antennae—their ability to connect, outfox, condemn, or console."[4]

Working Hand in Glove

The interesting relationship between the news media and politicians is like a dance that requires two partners. The news media need politicians and access for content. Politicians need the media to help spread their messages. They need each other for survival.

However, this relationship can also be antagonistic. In the 2008 presidential campaign, two reporters working for newspapers endorsing John McCain over Barack Obama were suddenly denied access to Obama's press plane.[5] The message was clear: if your employer endorses the other candidate, you lose access. To maintain their access to public figures, reporters and news outlets have to keep from upsetting them—which makes it incredibly difficult for journalists to do their jobs. So the focus shifts from investigative journalism to boosting ratings and raising advertising fees. And what ensures high ratings? Images and drama! Constant coverage and repetition, combined with our shortened attention spans, allow around-the-clock news cycles to turn any campaign mishap into a "story of the year."

During an Arab/Israeli conflict in the Middle East a few years ago, because I had never understood the background of the struggle, I asked a history teacher to explain it to me. When the teacher took a seat, I knew I was in for a long story. She said, "Well, it starts with Abraham. Yes, *that* Abraham." As previously discussed in the news chapter, context is often lacking. Politics and governance require so much contextual knowledge, yet the news media don't provide it to us. Perhaps that's our fault. After all, who would watch a two-hour special explaining the conflict in the Middle East? It's doubtful that such a broadcast would garner decent ratings. If anything is the least bit complicated or requires in-depth explanation, the news media will not offer it to us. They don't have the time, and we don't have the attention spans. As a result, political coverage focuses on superficial themes instead of policy positions. Policies are boring and unsexy, but reporting on what a female candidate wore to a certain event or how many homes a candidate owns entertains the masses. And what about covering what one candidate said about another candidate? You bet! Mudslinging is great for ratings.

"People used to complain that selling a president was like selling a bar of soap. But when you buy soap, at least you get the soap." —David Brooks

Media tries to make politics exciting by covering it like a sporting event, rather than actually talking about pertinent issues. *Attacked, volleyed, home run,* and *strikeout* have all been used to describe political debates. Campaigns are covered like a horse race, with candidates *pulling ahead* or *falling behind*. Political news coverage is

clearly about tactics and strategies. Let's face it; a *race* is more exciting than discussing real issues and analyzing policy, and the news
outlets know this.

Stacking the Deck

Another technique media uses to make political news exciting,
and the one that concerns me most, is using polls as actual news
material. Poll results can be manipulated, not only by the choice of
sample but also by how questions are worded. Look at the difference between these two questions that appeared in 1994:

> *"Do you think America should help the Bosnians defend
> their country?"*

> *"Should American men and women be deployed overseas to
> fight in Bosnia?"*

Whenever a pollster calls our house, I first ask them who paid
for the poll and who wrote the questions. Usually the caller says
she doesn't know, and I respond that I'll know after three questions
because, like those above, the questions are typically written so sub-
jectively that it's easy to determine the source and desired answer.

I'm not saying political polls should not be done; I'm saying poll
results should not be *news*. News outlets cover polls like they are
truth when, in fact, many of them have very few respondents. If
a poll relies on landline telephone calls, how many calls must be
made just to get a certain number of people to answer? Polls can
also be unreliable because the sample is generally weighted toward
conservative or liberal opinions. All of these faults make poll results
filler—not newsworthy. But because polls are used so heavily

during campaign seasons, they are a staple of the news diet, helping the writers create the "horse race" narrative that can affect an election. For example, if you hear from a poll that your candidate is way ahead, will you still make the effort to vote, or will you assume the race is already won? By contrast, if your candidate is way behind in the polls, will you skip voting because it's a lost cause? Both of these possible scenarios can impact voter turnout.

Money Matters

Politicians can raise staggering amounts of money during an election cycle, most of it used to buy campaign commercials. During every election, people complain about the negative, mean, and often misleading commercials candidates run about each other. And yet, these commercials continue to be produced and aired. Political commercials—and any lies contained within—are protected under the First Amendment as *political speech*. Broadcast stations are required to air them, even if they know the ads contain deceptions. However, given the money involved, I doubt refusing to air certain ads was ever a viable option. For example, local television stations collectively made $2.4 billion in political advertising in the 2014 election.[6]

"Selling the presidency like cereal! How can you talk seriously about issues with half-minute spots?" —Adlai Stevenson

Political commercials are some of the best examples of using appeals and the association principle. Positive ads about candidates are typically saturated with connotative images of America: the flag, babies, tractors, the Statue of Liberty, police officers, construction workers, brides, and grandmothers. Sound crazy? Look up Ronald Reagan's classic 1984 ad, *Morning Again in America*. When I show this ad in class and ask the students if they remember any of the voice-over statistics from the ad, they don't. The narration is irrelevant—the narrator could be reading a phone book. It's the images that resonate with us.

Negative ads use every possible production tool to create suspicion and anger. They're usually in black and white, the camera may zoom in on one particular image and then a fact—written in red, of course—will pop up on the screen, and the claims are usually stretched. And no warm narration this time; the voice is accusatory. For as much as people complain about negative ads, history proves they work. For example, in the 2012 presidential campaign, both Barack Obama and Mitt Romney spent over eighty-five percent of their ad funds—$791 million—on negative ads.[7] No one would spend this amount of money if negative ads did not have some effect.

Seeing Beyond Political Bias

Another issue with political news coverage is bias. As mentioned in the news chapter, bias can be obvious or as subtle as a connotative word in a photo caption. It can show up in the angle of a photo, the wording of a headline, or as an omission of some stories, and the open promotion of others. Complete objectivity may not even be possible when it comes to political coverage, and that's okay. Acknowledging bias exists is the first step toward rendering it ineffective. Remember selective exposure? There's a reason stations have certain political leanings; they are catering to their audience, giving them what they want.

Spotting bias in words or photos is fun and easy. It's more difficult to research institutional bias. In the 2014 political cycle, Fox News, the AP, CNN, *The New York Times*, *The Wall Street Journal*, *The Washington Post*, and *USA Today* all gave significantly more money to the Democratic Party than to the Republican Party.[8] While it's uncertain whether the personnel hired and newsroom viewpoints of these companies mirror those donations, it's worth studying.

How does one get valid political information in this media-saturated culture? I tell my students to get information from as many sources as possible and to never limit themselves to a single news source. Additionally, I encourage them to use their smartphones to research any claim made in a campaign commercial. The challenge is getting them to look past a candidate's image and research the candidate's stance on certain issues. The admonition to put in the time and effort to get the real story usually elicits a groan from the class. But the reward is being a well-informed voter and having the satisfaction of knowing they weren't duped based on image or misconception.

Why Promote Media Literacy?

"Media literacy is a quintessential skill that I am thankful to have learned. In our current society, we face a daily barrage of various media forms: billboards, television ads, pop-ups, magazines, and radio commercials. All of these make their way into our lives, whether we want them to or not." –*Ashley Cramer, former student*

Media Literacy at Home:

- What do we consider valid political information?

- Is it important to us what candidates look like?

- Are politicians under pressure from the media? Why?

- Which political issues do we actually care about?

- Are commercials a good way to learn about a candidate? Why or why not?

Media Literacy in the Classroom:

- Can you determine how much each vote costs a candidate?

- Predict how social media may have affected politicians from history.

- In what ways do old political commercials demonstrate the culture of that time?

- How can you evaluate the point of view of those who deliver political news?

- Which political issues should get more or less coverage?

QR CODES

**Political Media Fact Checker
–FactCheck.org**

**Clip: How Micro-Targeting Works
with Political Ads**

**"The Living Room Candidate"
–Library of Political Commercials**

FOOTNOTES

---

[1] Michael X. Delli Carpini and Scott Keeter, *What Americans Know about Politics and Why It Matters* (New Haven, CT: Yale University Press, 1996).

[2] Neil Postman, *Amusing Ourselves to Death: Public Discourse in the Age of Show Business* (1985; reprint, New York: Penguin Publishing, 2005), 45.

[3] Elihu Katz and Paddy Scannell, eds., *The End of Television? Its Impact on the World (So Far)* (Thousand Oaks, CA: SAGE Publications, 2009), 39.

[4] Steven Johnson, *Everything Bad Is Good for You* (New York: Riverhead Books, 2005), 103.

[5] Tom Ranstack, "Washington Times Kicked off Obama Plane," *Washington Times* (Washington, DC), October 31, 2008.

[6] "You Won't Miss Those Annoying Political Ads. Stations Will Miss the Money," *CNNMoney.com*, November 4, 2014, http://money.cnn.com/2014/11/04/media/political-ads-midterms/.

[7] "Mad Money: TV Ads in the 2012 Presidential Campaign," *Washington Post,* updated November 14, 2012, http://www.washingtonpost.com/wp-srv/special/politics/track-presidential-campaign-ads-2012/.

[8] Amy Chozick, "Donations by Media Companies Tilt Heavily to Obama," *Media Decoder* (blog), August 22, 2012, http://mediadecoder.blogs.nytimes.com/2012/08/22/donations-by-media-companies-tilt-heavily-to-obama/.

10

SEX, VIOLENCE, MONEY, AND MEDIA

FACTS TO REMEMBER:

- ☞ Six companies own ninety percent of the media.
- ☞ The universal appeal of sex makes it an effective hook.
- ☞ Violence in the media isn't inherently bad.
- ☞ It's important to analyze how messages in the media affect us.

The Perfect Storm: Sex, Violence, and Money

We've covered these topics in previous chapters, but, since these topics are the engines that run the media machine, I thought they deserved a little more attention. Sex and violence are the hooks used by the huge media companies to get and keep our attention, and they can also be the same hooks that keep certain news stories circulating.

If one were to create a news story guaranteed to get attention, the recipe would require a celebrity, some violence, perhaps some sexual aspects, and a load of money. Think of Ray Rice's elevator fight with his then-fiancée Janay Palmer. The story controlled news cycles for weeks. Why? Was it the celebrity? The violence and drama? The domestic violence angle? Or because the NFL generates over $1 billion in sponsorship revenue annually?

Once we are aware of how the media and news use the tools of sex and violence to grab our attention, it's easier to see "behind the curtain" and not get persuaded.

"People's misery becoming entertainment, that's what's dangerous. And that seems to be the place we're going. I worry about television." –George Clooney

Sex

Hello to those of you who turned to this chapter first because of the saucy title! And *thank you* for proving the point that sex has a universal appeal. Sexual content—pervasive in movies, music videos, television shows, and music lyrics—easily draws attention to any media production. That's why it's impossible to effectively analyze media without evaluating its use of sexual content.

Faced with competition from television, movies were the first to dabble in controversial topics. Fighting for ticket sales, movie producers told stories that television wouldn't touch. For example, the 1962 film *Lolita* about a middle-aged man's infatuation with a young girl, and 1971's *The Last Picture Show,* which included adultery, promiscuity, and alcoholism, both featured content that would have never been allowed on television. In fact, television in the 1950s was so *clean* that, even though they were married in real life, Ricky and Lucy Ricardo's characters in the classic series *I Love Lucy* slept in separate beds. Additionally, the show never mentioned the word "pregnant," even though Lucy, along with her character, truly was. Not until 1964 were married couples from *The Munsters* and *Bewitched* allowed to be shown in the same bed, but nothing beyond talking was allowed. (Perhaps, though, since it was Herman Munster, we should be grateful for that discretion.)

Fast-forward to the 1970s, and Maude Findlay, the namesake character of *Maude,* could not only say the word "pregnant," but she could also say "abortion"—and have one too. Programs continued to become more risqué, as shows like *The Love Boat* and *Dallas* included some sexual content in their themes. Once cable channels got involved, sexual portrayals on television took off and never looked back. From 1998 to 2005, sex scenes on television doubled. On average, music videos contain ninety-three sexual situations per hour, including eleven portraying intercourse and oral sex.

What's interesting is that, in 2005, only fifteen percent of the sexy scenes on television contained any mention of sexual responsibility or recourse.[1] The media portrays sex as easy, normal, and without consequences. So, although sexually suggestive themes and imagery can't be avoided when consuming media, if one were to depend on the media for sex education, his education would be sorely lacking.

We can't blame media producers for including sexy material. Their job, after all, is to make money for the stockholders. Nevertheless, many would say they have an obligation to show sexual situations responsibly. And while I agree media creators should show some restraint, it's naïve and idealistic to think they will do anything other than push the limits of society's moral standards. With all the media we consume, producers have to shock or thrill us to get attention; sex is frequently the bait that gets our attention.

"Mario will never start shooting hookers!" –George Harrison, Nintendo Co., Ltd.

Television, movie, and music producers aren't the ones using risqué imagery to turn our heads. Ever since Brooke Shields announced in 1980 that nothing came between her and her Calvins, Calvin Klein has been pushing the sexual boundaries in advertisements. But it's brilliant! Even if a Calvin Klein ad campaign is criticized and, better still, there is a threat of a boycott, Calvin Klein gets *free publicity* in the news. Even if an ad is pulled after negative publicity, it will live forever on the Web, creating more notoriety for the company. Truly, there is no such thing as bad publicity.

In my opinion, the pressure students feel to be sexually active correlates to the amount of media they consume. When I ask students to name one virgin on any television show currently in production, they're hard pressed for an answer. Lisa Simpson always gets mentioned, but after that, silence. The lack of virginity on television, at least when it's not the butt of a joke, normalizes sexual behavior and makes students think "everyone is doing it" when, in reality, teen sexual activity is down.[2]

The universal appeal of sex means it translates well into other cultures, although scenes may not have the same impact with every audience. Content that is considered sexually explicit in one country might seem tame to another. As a result, identifying what constitutes sexual activity within programs or ads is difficult. In fact, simply defining sexually explicit material is extremely challenging. Helping students become aware of how their perceptions about sex are being shaped by the media will empower them to step back. Perhaps, they'll realize all that heavy breathing isn't love or real life but an act to keep them watching and buying what advertisers are selling.

Violence

Google the terms *media* and *violence* and you get nearly eighty-seven million results. Everyone seems to have an opinion about what should be done about violence in the media. From a media literacy perspective, though, we can analyze violence in the media for its purpose, value (or lack thereof), and effect.

Comic books were once criticized as being too violent. A 1940 editorial in the *Chicago Daily News* claimed that "the effects of these pulp-paper nightmares is that of a violent stimulant…their hypodermic injection of sex and murder make the child impatient with better, though quieter, stories."[3] The editorial, written by Sterling North, was later picked up by dozens of newspapers around the country.

Criticizing violent media content did not begin with mass media. In fact, Beethoven's *Ninth Symphony* was criticized as "unspeakable cheapness" and one letter to the editor in London wrote, "The effect which the writings of Beethoven have had on the art must, I fear, be considered injurious."[4] Musician Gustav Leonhardt even considered it "vulgarity."[5]

"TV is the single most significant factor contributing to violence in America." –Ted Turner

Criticism of violence in electronic content then should come as no surprise. In 1950, Senator Ed Johnson criticized radio crime dramas and asked to include articles about them in the Congressional Record.[6] The FCC Chairman at the time, Wayne Coy, similarly criticized television after a survey found over one hundred murders and ten thefts portrayed on television in one week.[7] Considering the number of those portrayals has multiplied exponentially, can you imagine what Chairman Coy would think today?

Blaming electronic media for violence in society is easy and common. Simply examine the media coverage of any school shooting, and one of the first things discussed about the shooter is usually what movies he watched and what video games he played. But objectively analyzing violence in the media requires a thoughtful approach because violence itself is subjective. The word could be used in reference to physical violence, sexual violence, gun violence, emotional violence, or verbal or psychological violence. Our different definitions and views on what constitutes violence make evaluating it problematic.

To further confuse things, not all violence shown in media serves the same purpose. For example, sometimes witnessing violence in media prompts us to become emotionally involved or even compelled to action. A movie about child abuse could increase awareness of the issue. Violent or disturbing news clips from a natural disaster might be difficult to watch, but it could actually lead people to donate money or resources. An argument could be made that violence is sometimes necessary to tell a story. My mother, for example, thought *Apocalypse Now* was too violent and the language was offensive, but how could one make a movie about the war in Vietnam without including violence? *Saving Private Ryan* was also criticized for its brutal, graphic scenes of the D-Day landings, but how could Stephen Spielberg have told the story of the Allied invasion of Normandy without violence? Similarly, would a film about slavery that contained no violence whatsoever be realistic or socially responsible? In some cases, violence is a necessary part of the story.

Gratuitous violence, however, is different in that its only purpose is to keep consumers engaged or entertained. Violent acts are sometimes simply thrown into a media presentation without being a necessary part of the story. *South Park* parodies this by killing the Kenny character during every episode, only to have him reappear in the next episode to be killed again. No one makes fun of non-essential violence better than Itchy and Scratchy from *The Simpsons*. Sometimes the violence is so absurd it seems satirical. *The Bunnyman Massacre*, a 2014 movie, is described this way: "When a maniac in a rabbit suit embarks on a killing spree, a storekeeper sells the victims as beef jerky."[8] When I heard about *The Bunnyman Massacre*, I mistakenly assumed the horror film was a spoof that might have aired on Comedy Central. I was wrong.

Like sex, producers include violence in media presentations for economic reasons; it translates well into other languages. Think of this way: which type of conflict resolution would be best received in other countries—a detailed, dialogue-driven conversation, or a car chase complete with a gun battle? Explosions beat dialogue at the box office every time, in almost every culture. Violence means big profits for the huge multinational conglomerates that own and create our media. For years, critics have accused media makers of catering to the lowest common denominator when it comes to content. When it comes to violence, it seems the critics are correct.

Unlike the story of our friend in the bunny suit, in some cases, the violence isn't a part of any scripted drama or program. *America's Funniest Home Videos*, for example, is really nothing more than a collection of slapstick and people falling down. Additionally, a sad undertone, thoughtfully considered by *Los Angeles Times* writer Howard Rosenberg, accompanies this type of content: "What does matter is the show's undertone of sadism when it comes to children. Some comedy. What's funny about a toddler banging into a wall? Then another toddler doing the same thing? Then another? Then another?"[9]

This successful formula, though, exists in many programs, all the way back to Wile E. Coyote and the Road Runner. MTV's *Ridiculousness* clips make a viewer wonder if anyone was seriously injured, but we're never told because that would ruin the joke, and ABC's *Wipeout* even adds goofy sound effects to add to the fall's *punchline*. Is it any wonder people think we may be desensitized to violence? When it becomes something we laugh at, I think the answer is a definite *yes*.

Physician Mike Oppenheim actually thinks television *isn't violent enough*. In a famous essay he wrote for *TV Guide* in 1984, he states that viewers were surprised at how President Reagan reacted during his assassination attempt in 1981 because, unlike shootings portrayed in the media, he didn't immediately stumble and collapse after being shot. Oppenheim claims the media portrays violence as neat and clean, when, in reality, it is anything but. "Serious, real-life violence is dirty, painful, bloody, and disgusting...we don't need to clean up violence," he notes. "It's already too antiseptic."[10] In Oppenheim's view, realistic depictions of violence might act as a deterrent. Unfortunately, society's response is impossible to predict.

Blaming media violence for violence in society implies it did not exist before the mass media, but any basic knowledge of human history would disprove that. So there must be other variables leading to violence besides media consumption. After all, my classrooms have been filled with students who've consumed violent media for years, and, *so far*, they've been pretty well adjusted kids.

Video Game Violence

Video games tend to be a hot button issue when I talk about media violence to parent groups. And, yes, there are definitely some video games I would never buy for my sons. But for the most part, I'd prefer they play video games than watch television. If that sounds crazy, let me explain.

Watching TV is a passive experience. Someone else has written the story; there's no interaction with the media or other people. Television programs require nothing except my children's eyeballs. They are simply consumers of the product. Modern video games, however, offer a completely different experience. In many cases, my boys play in a "map" or online world they have personally created by planning, collaborating, and prioritizing—often with friends or cousins hundreds of miles away. They are solving puzzles, exploring, and are in charge of the narrative. The video game experience is not linear—it's different each time it's played. And I can't deny I get a rush of excitement when I see my boys working together to kill Nazis.

> ## "If a teenager can't discern right from wrong, I'm pretty confident it has little to do with whether he or she watches Buffy or plays violent video games."
> ## –Sarah Michelle Gellar

When we talk about video games in class, my students invariably share how they learned about the pioneers from playing *Oregon Trail* or learned about taxes and governing from *SimCity*. We might not realize how much our students and kids are learning when they are relaxed and "playing." My youngest built an entire sorting system, complete with conveyor belts, in *Minecraft*—after he learned to cross-pollinate trees using the same game. Anyone who claims video games are a waste of time is making a gross generalization. Nevertheless, there are some games I will never buy my sons, and I hope they never buy for themselves. Many of them involve gratuitous misogyny, sadism, prostitution, and crime. So although I'm generally a fan of video games, some of them do not pass the "mom test."

We can't blame violence in the media for all of society's ills, but we do need to be aware of its presence and purpose. Likewise, as responsible consumers, we must ask why gratuitous violence exists in media programs and what effect it has on each of us.

- Does it desensitize us?

- Do depictions of violence normalize it?

- Do producers of media have an obligation to show violence responsibly?

While we can't control media creators or outlaw the messages they broadcast, we can teach the students—as recipients of these messages—to be aware of how the media affects their thinking and behavior.

Concentration of Ownership

In 1983, *fifty* companies owned ninety percent of the media. Today, only *six* companies own nearly ninety percent of the media products we consume. Make no mistake, media is a business. Whether privately held or publicly traded, these profit-based companies peddle whatever messages reap the most revenue. While they might also do some charity work, these business leaders and stockholders do not have our best interests as consumers, voters, or humans at heart. Their primary concern is the bottom line.

As the owner of YouTube and its own sites and services, Google is on its way to joining the big six: Walt Disney, General Electric, NewsCorp, Time Warner, CBS, and Viacom. And since Google censors information in other countries to appease less democratic governments, we would be wise to ask if Google censors for our government as well.

The companies that own our media have the power to influence— even *control*—our culture by what they cover and (perhaps, even more importantly) what they do not. Since we know that media will only tell us stories that make them money, isn't it wise to stop and wonder what stories we are NOT being told?

The *Columbia Journalism Review* keeps an outstanding and current list called *Who Owns What* that breaks down the ownership of every media outlet in the country. For those wanting to be media literate, it's a bookmark worth saving.

QR CODES

No Long-term Link between Violence in the Media and Real-life Violence

Research Study: Video Games Don't Make Us Violent

Infographic: The Illusion of Choice

FOOTNOTES

[1] Dale Kunkel, Ph.D., Keren Eyal, Ph.D., Keli Finnerty, Erica Biely, and Edward Donnerstein, Ph.D, "Sex on TV," *A Kaiser Family Foundation Report*, November 2005, https://kaiserfamilyfoundation.files.wordpress.com/2013/01/sex-on-tv-4-full-report.pdf, 21.

[2] "Youth Risk Behaviors Surveillance," (Centers for Disease Control & Prevention, 2013).

[3] Jamie Colville, "The Comic Book Villain, Dr. Fredric Wertham, M.D.," *Seduction of the Innocents and the Attack on Comic Books*, accessed June 13, 2015, http://www.psu.edu/dept/inart10_110/inart10/cmbk4cca.html.

[4] Peter McNab, "The IEA Italia Event," *Nine Points Magazine* (December 19, 2013): n.p., url: http://www.ninepointsmagazine.org/the-iea-italia-event/.

[5] "Gustav Leonhardt," *The Economist*, January 2012.

[6] Senator Ed Johnson, speaking in 81st Cong., 2nd sess., *Congressional Record*. (March 14, 1950): S 3285.

[7] Ibid., 3479-3480.

[8] "The Bunnyman Massacre," *DIRECTV*, accessed June 13, 2015, https://www.directv.com/movies/The-Bunnyman-Massacre-aEJHdjlzWjZ4YWVvOXdXZ1NsK09wUT09.

[9] Howard Rosenberg, "The Sadness Behind 'Funniest Home Videos,'" *The Los Angeles Times* (Los Angeles), March 21, 1990.

[10] Mike Oppenheim, "TV Isn't Violent Enough," *TV Guide*, February 11, 1984.

Closing Thoughts

Media are not the enemy. They are simply privately held, profit-based corporations making money from our time and interest. Because there's *so much* time and *so much* interest, we need to step back occasionally and reflect on what this means.

Helping each other become aware of the media's influence is the first step, followed by analysis and evaluation. Being media literate doesn't mean you lose your ability to enjoy media consumption. In fact, you may enjoy it *more*.

We owe it to the young people in our lives to teach them the purpose and contexts behind the media they consume and create. They're growing up in a media-saturated world where the technology—and the rules—are changing every day. To assume they can navigate these waters without some critical thinking is a mistake.

I hope this book, *Media Literacy*, has served its purpose of making you, and your students and family, more aware of the challenges and benefits of having so many information and entertainment sources at our disposal. I encourage you to keep learning about how media interacts with and influences our lives. I'll leave you with some excellent media literacy websites and books to check out if you find yourself bitten by the media literacy bug. Simply being intentionally aware of what you're seeing and hearing changes your life. Trust me—once you start noticing things, you can't *stop* noticing.

Welcome to my world!

Media Literacy Websites Worth Checking Out

Common Sense Media

https://www.commonsensemedia.org/

Parent Previews

http://parentpreviews.com/

Center for Media Literacy

http://www.medialiteracy.com/

National Association for Media Literacy Education

http://namle.net/

My "Media Literacy Toolkit" for Teachers and Parents

http://www.livebinders.com/play/play?id=631246&backurl=/shelf/my

Frank Baker's Amazing Media Literacy Website:

http://www.frankwbaker.com/

Further Reading

Amusing Ourselves to Death: Public Discourse in the Age of Show Business by Neil Postman

The Shallows: What the Internet is Doing to Our Brains by Nicholas Carr

Media Literacy: Keys to Interpreting Media Messages by Art Silverblatt

I Live in the Future and Here's How it Works by Nick Bilton

Reality Bites Back: The Troubling Truth about Guilty Pleasure TV by Jennifer L. Pozner

The News: A User's Manual by Alain de Botton

Media Literacy by James Potter

Daily News, Eternal Stories: The Mythological Role of Journalism by Jack Lule

The Influencing Machine: Brooke Gladstone on the Media by Brooke Gladstone, illustrated by Josh Neufeld

The Culture of Connectivity by José van Dijck

Approaches to Media Literacy: A Handbook by Art Silverblatt, Jane Ferry, & Barbara Finan

Watch This, Listen Up, Click Here: Inside the 300 Billion Dollar Business Behind the Media You Constantly Consume by David Verklin and Bernice Kanner

Present Shock: When Everything Happens Now by Douglas Rushkoff

PURE GENIUS
Building a Culture of Innovation and Taking 20% Time to the Next Level
By Don Wettrick (@DonWettrick)

For far too long, schools have been bastions of boredom, killers of creativity, and way too comfortable with compliance and conformity. In *Pure Genius,* Don Wettrick explains how collaboration—with experts, students, and other educators—can help you create interesting, and even life-changing, opportunities for learning. Wettrick's book inspires and equips educators with a systematic blueprint for teaching innovation in any school.

LEARN LIKE A PIRATE
Empower Your Students to Collaborate, Lead, and Succeed
By Paul Solarz (@PaulSolarz)

Today's job market demands that students be prepared to take responsibility for their lives and careers. We do them a disservice if we teach them how to earn passing grades without equipping them to take charge of their education. In *Learn Like a Pirate*, Paul Solarz explains how to design classroom experiences that encourage students to take risks and explore their passions in a stimulating, motivating, and supportive environment where improvement, rather than grades, is the focus. Discover how student-led classrooms help students thrive and develop into self-directed, confident citizens who are capable of making smart, responsible decisions, all on their own.

DITCH THAT TEXTBOOK
Free Your Teaching and Revolutionize Your Classroom
By Matt Miller (@jmattmiller)

Textbooks are symbols of centuries of old education. They're often outdated as soon as they hit students' desks. Acting "by the textbook" implies compliance and a lack of creativity. It's time to ditch those textbooks—and those textbook assumptions about learning! In *Ditch That Textbook*, teacher and blogger Matt Miller encourages educators to throw out meaningless, pedestrian teaching and learning practices. He empowers them to evolve and improve on old, standard, teaching methods. *Ditch That Textbook* is a support system, toolbox, and manifesto to help educators free their teaching and revolutionize their classrooms.

50 THINGS YOU CAN DO WITH GOOGLE CLASSROOM
By Alice Keeler and Libbi Miller

It can be challenging to add new technology to the classroom but it's a must if students are going to be well-equipped for the future. Alice Keeler and Libbi Miller shorten the learning curve by providing a thorough overview of the Google Classroom App. Part of Google Apps for Education (GAfE), Google Classroom was specifically designed to help teachers save time by streamlining the process of going digital. Complete with screenshots, 50 Things You Can Do with Google Classroom provides ideas and step-by-step instruction to help teachers implement this powerful tool.

About the Author

Julie Smith is recognized nationally and internationally as a leading expert in media literacy. As a professor at both Southern Illinois and Webster University in St. Louis for the past 15 years, Julie specializes in media literacy, advertising analysis, social media, digital literacy, and Web 2.0 approaches. With digital media part of our daily lives, Julie makes a strong case for integrating media literacy in our schools and classrooms. She teaches audiences across the country how to access and utilize Web 2.0 tools, and she supports educators in understanding how to embrace and leverage new concepts, such as social media, rather than fear them.

Bring Julie Smith to Your School or Event

Julie Smith's highly sought-after keynotes, workshops, and professional development programs help educators, parents, and students alike make sense of our media-driven culture. Her insights will change the way you think about the world we live in today and the significant role you play in it! Her confident, engaging, and down-to-earth style ensures the information she shares is highly accessible to all participants and that people leave her workshops inspired to be a part of this digital revolution. Popular presentation topics include:

Media Literacy: The Time Is Now!

Your Kids Are Doing It, Why Aren't You...? The Truth about Social Media

Tackling Social Media Responsibility: One School's Story.

Using Cell Phones in Class... It's NOT the Coming of the Apocalypse.

Contact:

Email: heyjuliesmith@gmail.com

Twitter: @julnilsmith

Web: DaveBurgessConsulting.com/speaking

CPSIA information can be obtained
at www.ICGtesting.com
Printed in the USA
FFOW04n1106010616
24516FF